FAMILY THERAPY

DATE DUE

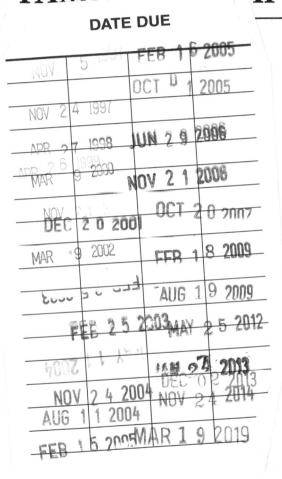

NOV 5 1997	FEB 1 6 2005	
	OCT 0 1 2005	
NOV 24 1997		
APR 27 1998	JUN 2 9 2006	
APR 26 1999		
MAR 9 2000	NOV 2 1 2006	
NOV	OCT 2 0 2007	
DEC 2 0 2001		
MAR 9 2002	FEB 1 8 2009	
FEB 2003	AUG 1 9 2009	
FEB 2 5 2003	MAY 2 5 2012	
MAY 1 2004	JAN 2 4 2013	
	DEC 0 2 2013	
NOV 2 4 2004	NOV 2 4 2014	
AUG 1 1 2004		
FEB 1 5 2005	MAR 1 9 2019	

BRUNNER/MAZEL
BASIC PRINCIPLES INTO PRACTICE SERIES

The *Brunner/Mazel Basic Principles Into Practice Series* is designed to present—in a series of concisely written, easily understandable volumes—the basic theory and clinical principles associated with a variety of disciplines and types of therapy. These volumes will serve not only as "refreshers" for practicing therapists, but also as basic texts on the college and graduate level.

1. Family Therapy: Fundamentals of Theory and Practice
   By William A. Griffin, Ph.D.

2. Essentials of Psychoanalysis
   By Herbert S. Strean, D.S.W.

**BRUNNER/MAZEL
BASIC PRINCIPLES INTO PRACTICE SERIES
VOLUME 1**

FAMILY THERAPY

Fundamentals of Theory and Practice

WILLIAM A. GRIFFIN, Ph.D.

BRUNNER/MAZEL Publishers • NEW YORK

Library of Congress Cataloging-in-Publication Data
Griffin. William A., Ph. D.
    Family Therapy : fundamentals of theory and practice / William A.
Griffin.
        p.   cm.— (Basic principles into practice series)
    Includes bibliographical references and index.
    ISBN 0-87630-719-5
    1. Family psychotherapy. I. Title. II. Series.
    [DNLM: 1. Family Therapy—methods.   WM 430.5.F2 G852f 1993]
RC488.5.G75   1993
616.89′156—dc20
DNLM/DLC
for Library of Congress   93-4316
                                                              CIP

Published by
BRUNNER/MAZEL, INC.
19 Union Square West
New York, New York 10003

Manufactured in the United States of America
10 9 8 7 6 5 4 3 2 1

Contents

Preface

PURPOSE OF THE BOOK

This book introduces the ideas, the concepts, and some of the techniques underlying family therapy. Some history is covered, but not much, and some people are introduced, but not many. The idea throughout this book is to broach a topic, discuss its relevancy and place in family therapy, and leave the reader with a trail of references.

How to Do General Family Therapy

Also included is a general discussion of how to do family therapy. The described approach is generic, and ahistorical. It combines the Communication (MRI, Strategic, Milan) and Structural schools, sprinkled with some behavioral and indirect hypnotic techniques. It reflects, I think, an amalgam of models typically seen in contemporary family therapy. It is not flashy, merely effective. Emphasis is on removing the presenting problem by altering the family's perspective of the problem and patterns of interaction.

When to Do Family Therapy

As you read these pages, it should become evident that, aside from a few rare situations, all child and adolescent problems should be treated as family problems. Child behavior problems do not occur in isolation. Hence, treating a problem as if it were in isolation simply forces the therapist to look for clues without benefit of context, insuring eventual failure.

For example, understanding the behavior of a child or adolescent is a lot like understanding the territorial behavior of a fish—repetitive behaviors or patterns make sense only after their function has been determined relative to the context in which the behavior occurred. This analogy illustrates the concept of ecological validity, and exposes a fundamental principle of family therapy.

The Family Unit

A theme throughout this book is that families function as a whole, they should be viewed as a whole, and they should be treated as whole. Learning how to view a family as a single entity is difficult. It requires abandoning most of the ideas about behavior, especially aberrant behavior, that were acquired during socialization. It is assumed that an individual's aberrant behavior, at any given time, reflects the composite state of the family system. At one level, this composite reflects the individual sub-units and their respective genetic and temperament contributions; at another level, it reflects how the family interacts internally, and how it buffers itself against society.

Level of the Reader

This book is written for several groups of readers. First, it can be used as a course text for an upper level undergraduate or a graduate course in Marital and Family Therapy. The text is simple, and it focuses on concepts rather than techniques. It has ample suggested readings to add depth and breadth.

Second, this text will be useful to the practicing professional who wants to, or is required to, learn family therapy. For such an individual, this book introduces family therapy as a concept rather than as a set of competing theories, each replete with a store of techniques and jargon. It attempts to simplify the idea of treating families, and to provide suggestions for additional readings as confidence, curiosity, and skills progress.

Introducing family therapy as a concept comes from many years of watching individual-oriented therapists apply individual techniques to multiple family members, and erroneously calling it family therapy. Or worse still, doing individual therapy with the identified client while other family members watch the proceedings. Treating the family as a single unit, irrespective of how many family members are present in the room, requires a perspective shift—a shift from viewing the behavior as reflecting an *individual's* entity versus viewing the behavior as reflecting a *system's* entity. In the first perspective, the individual is treated; in the latter, the relationship among system sub-units is treated. I have found that by teaching family therapy as a concept, not merely as techniques with theories attached, the necessary perspective shift occurs at a faster rate. Thus, the underlying emphasis throughout this text. However, to be a really good family therapist, you need to see families, read good professional books, attend seminars and meetings, and above all, get good supervision.

A conscious attempt is made to avoid specific terms or techniques. Instead the emphasis is on how to think about families and how to think about change. Theory is nice, but change is more important.

The concepts presented within the covers of this book reflect the author's biases. They are: (1) the presenting problem reflects the qualitative state of the immediate system in which the behavior is manifest, (2) the presenting problem should be removed, if possible, and (3) the therapist is responsible for altering the affective, behavioral, and cognitive patterns of the system so as to *allow* the behavior to be *unnecessary*.

What the Text Will Not Do

This text will not discuss in detail many of the current theoretical or philosophical battles that rage among the various family therapy models. Besides, much like a unique type of high-top basketball shoe, the popularity of the model will fade within a few years, only to be replaced by *new and improved* models. For example, although relevant, the Social Constructivist position will be discussed only tangentially. Similarly, while the Metaframeworks perspective (which attempts to combine theoretical apples and oranges into a palatable fruit salad) or the gender theories (e.g., Feminist theory) invite polemics and generate attention, they have yet to offer clear theoretical consistency or, more important, a better way of doing therapy.

Because of the intended audience, this book does not contain a section on research. As a researcher, I am compelled to comment occasionally on relevant process or outcome findings. Anyone wanting additional training in family therapy beyond this text should also become very familiar with the research literature. References for additional reading are noted throughout the text and in the Recommended Readings chapter.

Finally, this book purposely ignores the latest treatment trends (e.g., second-degree Post Traumatic Stress Disorder) and buzzwords (e.g., empowerment) in family therapy. While such intellectual food may feed some, as a teacher and researcher I am concerned only about treatment *effectiveness*. I have found that most trends come and go on a 3–4 year cycle, and few, if any, have had a demonstrative influence on therapy outcome. Fundamentally, family therapy exists not to sustain heuristic positions, but to improve the quality of life for individuals and families.

As you read this book, always keep in mind the *reality rule* of family therapy:

Therapy always progresses better in books and videotapes than in reality.

Acknowledgments

This book represents an accumulation of learning from my exposure to mentors, colleagues, and students. Some are pure clinicians, others are pure researchers, and still others attempt to bridge the gap between the two. Included among the mentors and colleagues are Russ Crane, Bill Gardner, John Gottman, Mavis Hetherington, Gerald Patterson, and Matt Stricherz. I have also been fortunate to have had a large number of students who have asked for (or demanded) concrete examples to complement my abstractions. These include: Fafar Guillebeaux, Laura Owens, Mary Madura, Maxine Cohen, Nancy Groppenbacher, and Shannon Greene. Additional thanks go to Shannon and Max for their help in the preparation of this manuscript, and to Nancy for her editorial comments.

I also want to thank my friend Maurice Azurdia for his willingness to take my thoughts and turn them into effective figures.

Of course, I am appreciative of the time and help extended by my own family. A special thank you is extended to Nancy Griffin for her continuous support throughout this project, and for her critical evaluation of the material in this book. And to Tagan and Tori who watched Daddy type, and type, and type.

FAMILY THERAPY

Fundamentals of
Theory and Practice

1

FAMILY THERAPY
A Shift in Perspective

FAMILY THERAPY: MODALITY VS PERSPECTIVE

Family therapy, done correctly, requires you to see the family as a single dynamic system. All parts interact with all other parts. No single action can have an isolated effect. Similarly, no single aberrant behavioral act can be thought of in isolation, nor is it simply a consequence of a string of behaviors. This act reflects a dynamic system internally configured to allow the behavior to be manifest. This idea of systems and interconnectedness is expanded later, although its introduction points to a unique feature of family therapy—specifically, family therapy is not a modality of psychotherapy, but rather a fundamental shift in perspective about the etiology of normal and aberrant behavior.

This chapter introduces to the reader the concept that family therapy requires the therapist to conceive of behavior as contextually based. Logically extended, this concept implies that treatment is also contextually based. Here context refers to the immediate environmental influences. Among these influences, interpersonal relationships, especially those in the family, are considered the primary vehicle for changing behavior—hence the rationale for family therapy.

ASSUMPTIONS ABOUT BEHAVIOR

Several assumptions about people, behavior, and change must be kept in mind as one makes the shift from an individual pathology model to a dynamic systems (i.e., interpersonal or interactional) model.

Most Behavior Is Nonpathological

First, very little of the behavior seen by most psychotherapists is pathological. As Torrey (1974) points out, most of the behaviors that therapists are asked to fix are simply problems of living. At any given moment the manifest behavior reflects the system's condition and, in general, how well the system is adapting to forces impinging on it. Most people come from families that adapt well, and produce only transitory adjustment problems.

Most Behavior Is Environmentally Driven

This perspective shift clearly moves the focus from the individual to the individual's context. With few exceptions, behavior is assumed to reflect environmental dynamics (see *Contraindications,* this chapter). How, when, and where a behavior occurs is determined by the history of the relationship between the behavior (or some variant of that behavior) and the environment.

When you adopt the position that environmental and contextual information drive behavior, then it follows that treatment implies altering the environment. This environment includes both the physical (behavioral sequences) and the perceptual (cognition; beliefs) aspects. More formally, you must assume that the behavior is a consequence of genetic composition coupled with current family patterns and history. In turn, this composite is coupled with, and reacts to, the larger social environment.

Families and Relationships Are Powerful Change Agents

Finally, arching above the assumptions about context, perception, behavioral sequences, and change is the fundamental assumption that families and relationships are the most potent change agents in an environment. (Colloquially referred to as the *Mother of All Assumptions*.) Hence, therapy occurs at the point of greatest therapeutic leverage—the family. Unlike demographers and census takers, therapists are not interested in whether the family is composed of individuals related by blood, marriage, or adoption. Instead, they focus on which relationships in the immediate environment affect the expression of behavior. Depending on the school of family therapy, this can include long dead grandparents or the 2nd grade school teacher (see Chapter IV: *Family Therapy Orientations*).

A CONCEPTUAL SHIFT

The pragmatic need to fix families inevitably leads to a single unifying concept of treatment: All therapeutic efforts should be directed toward the *relationship* among individuals, and not toward the individuals themselves. As family members interact, the composite of their interaction uniquely embodies the family. This composite is the object of therapy. This concept is shown in Figure 1.

This relationship among individuals refers to the processes that simultaneously reflect and dictate behavioral interactions. Key concepts are relationship and processes. Processes determine the relationship, and the relationship determines how processes occur. This is not a tautology. Relationship is a concept about quality, while processes are behavioral, cognitive, and affective patterns. Both occur simultaneously (i.e., processes reflect relationship), and their symbiotic relationship dynamically reconfigures as the system evolves over time. Family therapy is done with the relationship(s), and the thera-

THIS IS THE BASIC UNIT IN FAMILY THERAPY !!

Figure 1: Viewing family members and their interactions as the unit of treatment.

pist uses processes as the handles needed to affect and reshape the relationship.

To appreciate the processes necessary for a family to function well or badly, a conceptual shift must occur—moving from the individual deficit model to the interpersonal model. This shift allows the therapist to move away from the notion that the individual possesses the disorder, and to assume that the behavior reflects family interaction, history, and context. If this shift does not occur, the therapist is merely doing individual therapy with multiple people in the room.

The astute reader may be asking: If the individual is simply fulfilling an obligation within the system, is he or she responsible for the behavior that occurs? Yes. Irrespective of the assumed etiology, at the societal level the individual must be held responsible for any actions taken to fulfill the system obligation (Boszormenyi-Nagy, 1987).

Even if the individual is held responsible for the aberrant, abusive, or violent behavior, the therapist must separate the behavior from the function. Doing so allows you a better opportunity to observe current relationship features that endorse the behavior. If the child's behavior results from inadequate parenting or ongoing marital conflict, do not blame the mother; instead try to appreciate what permits the behavior to occur and what needs to change in order for the behavior to be unnecessary. Remember, that if you can discern what relationship or contextual features drive the dysfunctional behavior, then the behavior can be conceptualized as functional, making it easier to develop therapeutic strategies.

Therapy with the Relationship

From an interpersonal model, therapy involves a minimum of two entities: the therapist and a relationship. Initially, the most important question is, "Who or what is involved in the relationship?" Despite the implications of the term, family therapy does not need the entire family, but only those members necessary to alter the processes postulated to be influencing the presenting problem. Remember, only one person is absolutely needed, since the theory postulates that interactional changes reverberate throughout the system. Perspective is more important than the number of people in session.

In many cases, at least initially, having multiple family members present is helpful because the therapist has more opportunity to see relevant and nonrelevant patterns. It is analogous to the old football adage: First you tackle everybody, and then, one by one, throw bodies from the pile until you find the ball carrier. In the case of family therapy, instead of a ball carrier, you are looking for those interactional patterns that allow you the most leverage with the relationship. Each family member gives a slightly different perspective. In composite, the family brings multiple perspectives; the therapists must select one that is concrete, yet malleable, and fixable. This dilemma is portrayed in Figure 2.

Intangible relationships

Now let's extend the definition of a relationship beyond processes between two or more people to include processes between an individual and anything that can be interacted with or against. In other words, the interaction may be with some

Figure 2: Finding the relevant pattern among many.

person(s) or with some intangible object. This would include, for example, the way an individual interacts with a family myth (Bagarozzi & Anderson, 1989; Reiss, 1981), some preconceived notion of ideal family behavior, or history in the relationship (e.g., the proverbial, "He has always been like that!") or an attribution set (see Fincham & Bradbury 1990).

Stated differently, an individual does not necessarily need another living, breathing person to form a relationship with that produces dysfunctional behavior; a simple family myth is sufficient (see, e.g., Reiss, 1981). Note here that the individual is still not seen as having a deficit, even if the behavior is in reaction to a family myth. Instead, the focus is on the functionality of the behavior within the context of the myth. Hence, therapy is guided toward altering the relationship between the individual and the myth in order to allow the behavior to be unnecessary.

Conversely, you should also consider the situation where the individual conveniently maintains a myth in order to justify the behavior. Usually, this takes the form of, "I can't because . . ." For example, a mother with an acting-out adolescent 14-year-old daughter reported that she could not be expected to set and follow through on parenting guidelines because of her temper. In her words, "If I tell her once and she doesn't do it—I just lose it! It's my temper, I can't control it, and I've always had it." In this case, the mother did not want the responsibility of being a parent. Her temper was selective; it was uncontrollable only around parenting. By failing to parent, the mother insured that the girl's dysfunctional behavior would accelerate, guaranteeing that she would be sent back to residential treatment, which had been her home for the previous four years.

Behavioral Repertoire

In general, the behavioral acts that constitute the presenting problem are irrelevant. That is, it does not matter if Johnny's presenting problem is starting fights, engaging in oppositional behavior, or pulling out his hair. Only the assumption that the behavior represents a dysfunctional system is important.

Moreover, whether the behavior reflects poor parenting skills or failed solutions, or is a metaphor for the system dysfunction is less important than is the assumption that the behavior reflects interpersonal dysfunction somewhere in the system. In short, for the family therapist, the behavioral act is secondary to the processes that generate it. This is not to suggest that the behavior may not be hurtful, or dangerous to self and others, but rather that its function, and not the behavioral act itself, interests the family therapist.

Behavior brought to therapy as the presenting problem represents end-stage phenomena. You should assume that there had been smaller, less extreme unsuccessful behaviors occurring prior to the point of referral. Only after the less extreme behaviors fail does the behavior escalate sufficiently to warrant attention. In general, the behavior selected by a child or adolescent depends on the efficacy of the behavior relative to its function within the system. To truly appreciate the role of a behavior, it is better to see it as necessary than to see it as abnormal. In essence, kids use what works, and what works depends on what gets noticed by those in the immediate environment.

Behaviors representing a dysfunctional system can be crudely assessed across two dimensions: age appropriateness and degree of persistence. Age appropriate means that the child and the adolescent typically do what most kids that age do. If the adolescent acts like a younger child, or a younger child engages in adolescent behavior, then assume greater system dysfunction. Similarly, if the behavior is age appropriate, but the degree is extreme, assume greater system dysfunction.

Furthermore, any singular behavioral act is meaningless. It is only after a sustained pattern that the behavior warrants consideration as an indicator of system dysfunction.

Otherwise, assume the child is learning how to accommodate to social rules. For example, normal behaviors include defiant acts like saying no, or attention-getting behaviors in public (e.g., a three-year-old strategically flinging himself on the floor of the grocery store in front of the candy section). Also included is age-appropriate acting out, such as classroom behavior that is disruptive, or out-of-seat behavior. If such behavior becomes too disruptive or, as the child gets older, you see exaggerated risk-taking behavior, it may reflect system dysfunction. In boys, for example, normal adolescent fighting might become too frequent. For both boys and girls, normal adolescent experimentation of the big three (drugs, alcohol, sex) might exceed the experimentation levels. Conversely, lack of any experimentation probably means that the system lacks flexibility to allow age-appropriate individuation. The qualitative nature of deviant behaviors changes with age; saying no as a child is metamorphosed into refusing to eat in an anorectic adolescent. This evolution of this skill is illustrated in Figure 3.

FAMILY THERAPY

What Is Family Therapy?

Family therapy is any attempt to modify salient environmental features, most importantly interpersonal contacts or beliefs about those contacts, that alters interaction patterns, allowing the presenting problem to be unnecessary. Notice that this definition of family therapy does not necessarily exclude nonfamily members, nor does it necessitate that all family members be present in therapy (see Torgenrud & Storm, 1989).

Family therapy occurs through social negotiation. It involves determining what the family wants, how they see the problem, how they want it fixed relative to what you think is wrong, and what is within your capacity to alter.

Once an agreement has been negotiated, the therapist allows the presenting problem to be unnecessary by altering the family structure, which simultaneously alters interaction patterns, relationships, and beliefs about the family. Or alternatively, the therapist alters the beliefs about the relationship, which simultaneously alters patterns of interaction, and the family structure. Simply said, the therapist enters the family at the relationship level, not at the level of a particular individual, and alters how the various relationships are carried out.

At 8

At 11

At 18

Figure 3: Age-consistent displays of resistance to authority.

CONTRAINDICATIONS

Despite the widespread, almost evangelical endorsement of family therapy in the last decade, it is not the ideal treatment for all presenting problems with children. In particular, it is no more effective than any other form of psychotherapy for disorders having a genetic or organic basis. Here I refer to genetic basis as determined by empirical evidence accumulated with *some* degree of consistency. Fortunately, the list is short, and the average practicing psychotherapist will have infrequent contact with these groups. For example, these would include autism, schizophrenia, and bi-polar depression (see Rutter et al., 1990).

Several comments can be made about the above list. First, some readers may find that the list is too short and that their favorite disease is missing. Despite media attention, very few diseases, especially those characterized by psychological or behavioral symptoms, show a ***clear*** genetic pattern or physiological basis. Second, even in this short list there is controversy. For example, bi-polar depression was thought previously to manifest itself only in early adulthood or late adolescence, but with the onset of private psychiatric hospitals and more comprehensive health insurance, the age of initial diagnosis has plummeted, and the sale of lithium has increased—all this without evidence that the disease itself has changed, or even that the disease has a genetic basis (see Breggin, 1991, for an excellent review of the issues). Similar scientifically supported positions have been forwarded suggesting a lack of genetic evidence for autism (see, e.g., Sanua, 1986) and schizophrenia (see, e.g., Lewontin, Rose, & Kamin, 1984).

It should also be noted that while family therapy is not effective in altering the prognosis for biologically based disorders, there is accumulating evidence that family therapy is an excellent adjunct to standard pharmacological treatment. This is especially true for schizophrenia using the Psychoeducational model (see Chapter IV: *Family Therapy Orientations*). Finally, while the individual deficit model views aberrant behavior as being internally generated, the interpersonal model assumes that such behavior reflects the dynamic interaction between learned rules (via the family) and the immediate context. Extended further, the interpersonal model views violent or bizarre behavior as resulting from strategies that successfully evolved and were reinforced within the system (Patterson, 1982). Unfortunately, as empirical evidence suggests, after standing patterns are concretized, they are not amenable to any form of treatment, family therapy or otherwise (Kazdin, 1987; Patterson, Reid, & Dishion, 1992).

SUMMARY

This chapter provides a general overview of the thinking that supports family therapy. Several points are absolutely necessary to grasp:

- You treat the relationship, not the individual. Relationship refers to the pattern (affective, behavioral, cognitive) between the individual and whomever or whatever that individual is interacting with.
- The conceptual shift from an individual deficit model to a relationship model is the most difficult part of becoming a good family therapist.
- Assume that all behavior occurs within a context, and that context determines what you do in therapy.
- The breadth of perspective for the family therapist is more important than the number of people in the therapy session.

2

INTRAPERSONAL VS INTERPERSONAL MODELS

INTRAPERSONAL VS INTERPERSONAL MODELS

Intrapersonal Model

Family therapy is an *interpersonal* model of psychotherapy; it focuses on treating the *relationships* among members of a delimited environment. On the other hand, traditional psychotherapy is an *intrapersonal* model of psychotherapy; it focuses on treating the assumed structural *deficit* within the individual. The individual deficit model has a long and illustrious history. Although this model did not begin with Freud, he certainly was a strong advocate (Fenichel, 1945).

Interpersonal models of psychotherapy and the individual deficit models hold distinct assumptions about psychopathology, and behavior change. Among the differences, two are particularly influential in the treatment of psychological disorders in childhood. These two are: the assumption of individual psychological deficit, and the hydraulic notion of behavior.

Individual deficit assumption

A clear and consistent message implicit in traditional psychotherapy is that the individual with the presenting problem has a core deficit. This person either lacks skills (*behavioral*), has skewed thinking (*cognitive*), or is developmentally arrested or unable to resolve internal conflicts (*psychodynamic*). Irrespective of etiology, the problem is within the individual. Usually, the theories refer to some nebulous entity like character flaw or inadequate ego. Irrespective of the psychological construct chosen to support the theory, the very act of naming it implies a true and legitimate entity. This entity is referred to in much the same manner as the heart or spleen, or any other organ of the body.

From this flawed-component model, it makes sense that traditional psychotherapy techniques, except some forms of behavioral models, are employed as if the individual operated in a contextual vacuum. Although most theories mention the environmental influences, it is usually with respect to how the environment provides an opportunity for the client's deficit to manifest itself. Such a narrow focus allows the therapist to label the individual according to ever changing social and political nomenclature (e.g., DSM-IV), and to maintain that the label reflects a constitutional weakness in the individual.

Hydraulic notion of behavior

Freud, like any observer of human nature, interpreted contextual relationships consistent with the prevailing views of the period. In the case of Freud, he was a product of the *Physicalism* movement in the mid-nineteenth century, and the *Naturphilosophie* movement of the early nineteenth century (Holzman, 1970). The *Naturphilosophie* movement, a philosophical-theological model, holds that the world can be understood intuitively as an immense system where internal forces and activities constantly battle to emerge and change form. From this Freud concluded that man, and all of his parts, are involved in this constant emergence. For Freud, the idea of internal conflict and continual emergence had a pervasive influence on his thoughts about the motivation of behavior.

Among the European intellectuals, *Naturphilosophie* was replaced by *Physicalism*, an extreme swing toward a strict mechanistic and quantitative view of the world. From this world view Freud took, among other things, the notion of force (energy), and energy conservation and expenditure (Holzman, 1970). As Freud began speculating about the etiology of Hysteria, his early readings of *Naturphilosophie* and *Physicalism* seemed to provide the needed answers.

Unfortunately, the answers he derived were mired in these narrow perspectives. For example, from the *Naturphilosophie* approach Freud pulled the concepts of internal and continuous conflict, and from the *Physicalism* approach he utilized the ideas of the energy expenditure and regulation. These philosophical positions provided a rationale for "letting off steam," and other euphemisms for the benefit of and implicit necessity for energy release. Moreover, and especially relevant to current abreaction techniques in traditional psychotherapy, Freud was also influenced by the then prevalent idea in neurology that periodic discharge was needed to regulate (i.e., re-establish optimal levels) organismic tensions brought about by external stimulation of an otherwise passive organ (nerves) (Holzman, 1970).

From these early notions of energy discharge and regulation, individual psychodynamic psychotherapy and its more contemporary cousins (e.g., gestalt), have expounded the therapeutic benefits of catharsis, abreaction, and emotional expression. A consequence of this line of thinking is that affect expression should somehow be considered superior to either cognition or behavior. The desire for affect expression, especially crying or any abreaction during a session, is supported by the theoretical assumption that the crying somehow re-establishes the energy equilibrium and, therefore, must be therapeutic. Despite the lofty position enjoyed by affective expression, there is scant evidence that it has therapeutic effectiveness greater than other therapy models that advocate either cognitions or behaviors (Gurman, Kniskern, & Pinsof, 1986). And in some situations, affect expression may be detrimental. For example, with violent couples, emphasis on affect expression increases the risk for subsequent abuse (Strauss, 1974).

Interpersonal Model

Unlike the individual deficit model, family therapy has as a basic premise that behavior at any given instant reflects the quality of the environmental system. Moreover, and relative to the individual deficit model, family therapy assumes, a priori, that the individual expressing a symptom for the system is no more or less likely than any other family member to be psychologically vulnerable. Simply put, the identified patient is fulfilling a role within the larger system.

As discussed in Chapter IV: *Family Therapy Orientations*, each model in family therapy proposes a different reason for the dysfunctional behavior. Some assume multigenerational process, while others assume psychological remnants from attachment figures, and still others assume a skills deficit in the parent. Although each model has different assumptions about the behavior, a single conceptual thread binds them together—the identified patient (IP) represents the cumulative inability of the immediate environment, usually the family, to functionally adapt to exogenous or endogenous changes that naturally occur as a system evolves over time. Furthermore, while the family produces the symptom, the IP is simply selected as the carrier; this implies that any sibling could do just as good a job if drafted for duty.

The idea that the behavior of individuals reflects their adaptation to the family system is not new. It has been discussed in some form for decades. In psychiatric writings, an early proponent for this idea was Harry S. Sullivan (1953). Unlike Freud, Sullivan was quick to point out that the interaction between mother and child determines how the child subsequently interacts with others. This interpersonal school of psychoanalytic thinking, however, falls short of discussing current behavior, only discussing how the early interactions shaped the personality structure (i.e., deficit) in the presenting patient.

Most schools of individual psychotherapy evolved as splinter groups from a main line of theoretical thought. Family therapy, on the other hand, did less evolving and more converging. Specifically, early practitioners (1940s–1950s) in the field (John

Bell, Nathan Ackerman, Murray Bowen) were seeing patients and their families conjointly for various, usually disparate, reasons. Bowen, for example, involved families as part of treatment for childhood schizophrenia, whereas Ackerman viewed psychopathology as a result of intrapersonal and interpersonal conflict within the family. Although in the mid 1950s several maverick psychiatrists, psychologists, and social workers were working with the family as a vehicle to treat the presenting client, there was no theoretical glue to bind the movement. Slowly, through the dissemination of papers, and meetings in hotel bars during conferences, several common rationales for "why to see families" began to emerge based on a common metaphor—the family as a system.

Once a common metaphor was agreed on, the next step was to find a theory consistent with the metaphor, yet sufficiently vague to allow the individual practitioners to interpret the tenets of the theory consistent with their current practice. After about a decade, two similar theories came to the forefront, General Systems Theory and Cybernetics. Information Theory, albeit less visible, also had an influence on the early practitioners in family therapy.

General Systems Theory

Of all the influences in family therapy, none have received the praise and the critical dissection given to General Systems Theory (GST). Originally forwarded by the biologist Ludwig von Bertalanffy in the early 1930s, this theory proposes that a system is any organization of interacting parts having a purposeful outcome (von Bertalanffy, 1968). This includes biological, mechanical, sociological, or psychological organizations. Families obviously fit this definition. Another prominent feature of this theory is the assumption that the "whole is greater that the sum of its parts." For the clinician, this dictates the idea that treatment should focus on the organization of subunits, rather than on dissecting the sub-units that compose the system.

Since General Systems Theory is applicable to all scientific disciplines, each has adopted its own interpretation of the theory. In the family area, not surprisingly, it is called Family Systems Theory. Of the hundreds of articles and books written about family systems theory, a few are penetrable, and do not induce immediate sleep; among the best is a chapter by (Steinglass, 1987). According to Steinglass (1987), Family Systems Theory has three core concepts: (1) organization, (2) morphostasis, and (3) morphorgenesis. Within each concept there are several subconcepts that are relevant to therapists. These are outlined in Table 1.

These are only a few of the many concepts generated by the General Systems Theory. Good sources of information are: Buckley (1967); Davidson (1983); Gray, Duhl, and Rizzo (1969); Maruyama (1963); Wynne (1984); and von Bertalanffy (1968).

Cybernetics

Cybernetics, like GST, is a general theoretical model advocating the interrelatedness of parts within a functioning entity. This model was developed by Norbert Weiner, an MIT mathematician, while working for the government during World War II. Weiner was part of a post-W.W.II movement that sought to advance scientific thought and social good by viewing the world in terms of a defined entity composed of interdependent parts. While von Bertalanffy relied on biological terms to describe his work, Weiner (1961) relied on mechanical terms to describe the properties of a system. In many respects, GST and Cybernetics are indistinguishable, and need not be otherwise for the practicing clinician. General introductions to Cybernetics can be found in Ashby (1956) and Weiner (1961).

A Cybernetic term employed by family therapists is *feedback loop*. Feedback loop refers to information about the state or quality of the system that is entered back into the system and used to adjust subsequent output. The utility of a feedback loop for assembly line quality control is obvious, but understanding its role in the family is not. In simple terms, feedback loops in family therapy refer to how families react behaviorally to a given set of circumstances, either unexpected (e.g., adolescent pregnancy) or developmental (e.g., child enters school). If

Table 1
Key Concepts of General Systems Theory

Concept	Subconcept and Definition	Clinical Relevance
<u>Organization</u>: elements of a system are organized and predictable		
	<u>Wholeness</u>: the family forms a single entity with its own characteristic	Conceptually, individual behavior simultaneously determines and is determined by the family
	<u>Boundaries</u>: family members are bounded by time and space	Describes the internal construction, and degree of separation among family members
	<u>Hierarchies</u>: hierarchical arrangement of the family	Describes the power structure (parent in control) in the family
<u>Morphostasis</u>: families behave in a stable and predictable manner		
	<u>Homeostasis</u>: the property used to maintain consistency in structure during periods of change	Resiliency in the face of change; often, incorrectly labeled resistance by unsuccessful therapist
<u>Morphorgenesis</u>: the ability of the family to change as situation dictates		
	<u>Feedback loops</u>: (cybernetics term) use of information in self-correcting behavior in reaction to environmental (e.g., house fire) or familial (e.g., a birth) changes	Positive feedback exacerbates the reaction to the changes (usually wrong thing to do), and negative feedback dampens the reaction (usually good thing to do)

the reactions are extreme and exacerbate the problem, the feedback loop is considered positive (increases reaction), or if the reactions are moderate and stabilize the system, the feedback loop is considered negative (dampens the reaction).

Information Theory

The often unacknowledged theory behind family therapy thinking, especially the Communication school (e.g., MRI), is Information Theory (Shannon & Weaver, 1949). Although the concepts inherent in this theory (e.g., channel capacity, information redundancy, entropy [also from GST]) abound in family therapy theory, explicit reference to the theory is scant. Developed by Claude Shannon at Bell Labs in the late 1940s, Information Theory describes the process, and the probability, of non-errored communication, both eminent concepts in early family therapy theory development (see, e.g., Bateson et al., 1956; Watzlawick, Beavin, & Jackson, 1967). General introductions to Information Theory are Attneave (1959) and Darnell (1972).

For the practicing clinician, Information Theory is relevant for one major reason: It emphasizes how information is sent and received, and how it varies as a function of the system's capacity to transmit with minimum error. Errors in human interaction typically result from cognitive sets or filters that are cumulative and contain bias. This bias, both its valence and amount, simultaneously reflect and determine the existing quality of interpersonal relationships.

INCONGRUENCE: INTRAPERSONAL VS INTERPERSONAL MODELS

As repeated often in this book, the conceptual difference between an interpersonal model and an individual deficit model is the most difficult transition a practicing family psychotherapist has to make. Below are a series of theoretical assumptions that highlight the differences between relationship-based family therapy models and individual deficit models. These are middle ground positions. Some family therapy orientations are more radical in their conceptualization of differences, some less.

Etiology and Spontaneous Change

Individual deficit models assume, at least theoretically, to know how or why the presenting problem probably began. Typically, and depending on the orientation, it may be unresolved conflicts, single traumatic events, or residual conflicts and attachments to parental figures. In contrast, the interpersonal model assumes only that the presenting problem represents the current manifestation of the system dysfunction. This outward manifestation reflects a conjunction of behavior and time in the system's evolution. As such, it assumes that there is no single etiological agent, nor does it assume even that relevant event(s) can be reliably identified. It is not surprising, then, that according to this model, etiological information is unnecessary for successful treatment.

Also, since the manifestation of the present problem is temporally connected to the state of the system, there is acknowledgment that some proportion of families will spontaneously get better. Equally as plausible, symptom expression can be passed from one child to another when, for example, the original child goes to college or is put in residential treatment.

Contrast this with the individual deficit perspective that assumes that the character flaw is always present, and its manifestation depends only on the opportunity to express itself. Notice further that this character flaw scenario warrants the use of diagnostic labeling (that is, aside from insurance reimbursement) and provides utility for the terms latent, manifest, transformation, and sublimation. In effect, spontaneous improvement (i.e., absence of deficit) is impossible without active remedial steps (e.g., psychotherapy), and any disappearance of the presenting problem assumes that the deficit is present but latent or, better still, has been sublimated into an acceptable hobby.

Longitudinal vs Cross-sectional Perspective

From a systems perspective, the presenting problem indicates the state of the system assessed from a cross section in time. Relevant behaviors can fluctuate as the system changes. Though it seldom does, the presenting problem can change rapidly or move to a different member of the family depending on the movement within the system.

Conversely, the individual perspective sees the presenting problem as the inherent flaw or structural defect in the organism expressed over time. This individual model with a longitudinal perspective would not predict changes across family members, nor radical changes in the diagnostic label applied to the individual's behavior.

Client Resistance

In general, client resistance, at least according to the individual deficit model, is "the individual's conscious or unconscious psychological defense against bringing repressed (unconscious) thoughts to light" (American Psychiatric Association, 1975). In other words, the client is at fault for not responding to treatment. On the other hand, family therapy views resistance as a natural response to a request for change. Resistance reflects family homeostasis (see Table 1). This regulatory mechanism is essential to the perpetuation of the system. Thus, resistance, a manifestation of homeostasis, is neither good nor bad, but can be expected to some degree in most attempts to change long-standing behavior patterns. It provides information about the system structure and organization. In most cases, resistance is temporary, and the information gained from the resistance is used to develop subsequent interventions. It is most likely to appear following multiple sessions of demonstrated therapist incompetence, laziness, or lack of imaginative tasks.

Conversely, good therapists are often designated as such based simply on their ability to anticipate and utilize this homeostatic property. Much of the published work of Milton Erickson emphasizes the importance of incorporating anticipated resistance into the therapy plan (see, e.g., Zeig, 1980). Assume, for example, that among the family members the father will be the most reluctant to try the new prescribed behavior. You could prescribe this reluctance and then swiftly nudge him to change, by saying, "Dad, I realize that you and Johnny have had many battles recently, and like most men with pride, you're not about to change too quickly. That's O.K., you can take no longer than absolutely necessary to demonstrate to Johnny that his attempts to frustrate you have been successful."

Failure to change a presenting problem also results from the individual not wanting patterns to change, although expressing otherwise. Though rare, it usually occurs when there are reasons for being in therapy other than those explicitly stated. One spouse, for example, may be planning to leave the marriage and wants the other spouse and child in therapy when it happens. But in general, family resistance should be thought of as an opportunity to better understand the organizational rules of the family (see Anderson & Stewart, 1983; de Shazer, 1984; Steinglass, 1987).

Psychometric Testing

Although assessing the relationship between physical impairment (e.g., eyesight) and acting-out behavior in children and adolescents is worthwhile, from the perspective of the interaction model, standard psychometric tests (MMPI, CPI) have little value for clinical evaluation and treatment. Such tests are residuals from an individual deficit, medical model perspective. Information provided by these tests provides little that is useful for treating the relationships that generate the dysfunctional behavior. All relevant information is obtained through clinical interview. In fact, giving such tests to an individual wrongly implies that the individual possesses the disorder. To subsequently call the procedure family therapy is logically inconsistent and, typically, a failure. If instruments must be given for practical reasons (e.g., insurance, research), these should measure family dynamics at the relationship level, not at the individual level. For example, at the couple level, the Locke-Wallace Marital Status Test should be used (see Crane, Allgood, Larson, & Griffin, 1990).

The Value of History

Depending on which orientation you choose, history may or may not be valuable. If, for example, the therapist has a multigenerational perspective (e.g., Bowen, 1978), then history is important as a means for constructing the transmission of dysfunction. Conversely, the communication models (e.g., MRI) need very little history before proceeding with therapy. In general, the position of the systems perspective is that history may or may not have influence on current behavior, but it unequivocally maintains that recalling past events has little value in changing current behavior (Haley, 1973). Moreover, proponents of this perspective would argue that the past is recalled as a function of the therapist questions. The questions are based on training and theory. Answers to the questions are interpreted to confirm the hypotheses that initially generated the questions, hence confirming the theory (and incidentally reaffirming the value of those long years of graduate training). In effect, questions about history confirm theoretical leanings.

Most individual deficit models assume that discussion of history somehow restores or repairs some portion of the deficit. Interpersonal models also fall into the same theory -> question -> confirmation trap, but with one difference. Since interpersonal models assume no individual deficit, then questions focus on patterns, not history. This alternate focus allows the family or individual an opportunity to view the behavior differently (e.g., external, controllable) and, along with therapeutic tasks, provides the means for changing behavior.

Catharsis; Abreaction

Abreaction refers to "emotional release or discharge resulting from recalling to awareness a painful experience that has been forgotten because it was consciously intolerable" (American Psychiatry Association, 1975). Unlike the individual deficit model that evolved from Naturphilosophie, Physicalism, and the industrial revolution, that has conflict and energy regulation as basic tenets, the interpersonal model assumes no internal conflict nor a therapeutic need to cathart, or to demonstrate abreaction. As such, very few of the primary family therapy models advocate the therapeutic value of affective expression, but they do not specifically discourage it. For example, the Bowenian model emphasizes cool rationalism, Structural is indifferent, and the Experiential approaches view affect expression as necessary, but not sufficient for system change. As a general position, any spontaneous affect expression is considered normal in all human interaction, but affect void of behavior change has no unique therapeutic value.

Defense Mechanisms

Defense mechanisms, defined as "unconscious intrapsychic processes serving to provide relief from emotional conflict and anxiety" (American Psychiatric Association, 1975), are theoretically consistent with the individual deficit model, but are logically at odds with the interpersonal model. First, since interpersonal models attend to interpersonal patterns, the unconscious versus conscious dichotomy is irrelevant; not because family therapists are averse to the idea (see, e.g., Haley, 1973), but since the goal of therapy is not to bring the unconscious to the realm of conscious, time is better spent working on system patterns. Second, behaviors that previously were ascribed to defense mechanisms (i.e., character flaws) are seen by family therapists as simply behaviors fulfilling a role within the familial system.

Reframe vs Interpretation

Reframing is a cornerstone in the ahistorical approaches in family therapy. Reframing occurs when the therapist takes the presenting problem or dysfunctional situation and *offers* the family or individual an alternative perspective other than the one brought to therapy. Relative to the perspective brought by the family, this reframed perspective will vary along four dimensions. First, the reframe removes the notion of an individual deficit. Second, it elevates the dysfunction to the system level. Third, it invokes a different connotation (e.g., junior's hitting of sister was not due to a chemical imbalance, as you were informed by the TV talk show, but rather was his way of letting you know that you have not being spending time with him). And, finally, the new perspective is amenable to treatment.

Reframing is negotiation. In effect, the therapist gathers information and puts a "spin" on the data (i.e., creates a new story) in such a way that the solution to the problem is slightly different. It removes blame, involves multiple people, and, most importantly, is solvable. Often, families are hesitant to accept the new perspective, and linguistic sparring occurs until a join agreement is reached by all parties. Usually, the family fights to retain some portion of their story, and the therapist extracts a presenting problem amenable to treatment. Two points should be emphasized: (1) reframes involve subtle negotiation of perspective, followed by an agreement, and (2) the final agreement contains a presenting problem amenable to treatment.

Conversely, interpretation, as employed by individual therapists, is the process of communicating to the patient understanding of a particular aspect of his problems or behavior (American Psychiatric Association, 1975). Stated differently, interpretations reflect the therapist's conviction about the unconscious meaning of certain behaviors or utterances. The common feature across these two definitions, as well as the single most powerful characteristic that differentiates an interpretation from a reframe, is that interpretations are offered as being *factually based and correct* (see Fisher & Greenberg, 1985, for a detailed discussion). In effect, in the individual deficit model, interpretations are offered by a learned psychotherapist as insights into behaviors. If the client disagrees with the interpretation, the client is termed resistant or lacking in the capacity for insight. Either way, the therapist is correct and the client has the deficit. On the other hand, a reframe of the presenting problem, if done correctly, provides an opportunity for a collaborative perspective via negotiation.

Psychopathology, Diagnosis, and the Latest DSM

Even the most ardent applied geneticists concede that genetic predisposition is seldom sufficient for the manifestation of a disorder (see, e.g., Gottesman, 1991; Konner, 1982; Plomin, 1989; Rutter, Macdonald, Le Couteur, Harrington, Bolton, & Bailey, 1990). Given the current knowledge of genetics and the imprecise measurement of psychological disorders, a good working position assumes that behavior is a dynamic interaction between physical features, psychological predisposition (e.g., temperament), and environment. In this composite, environment includes culture, economic and social conditions, and the family. The interpersonal position assumes that the family system, with its ability and mode of adaptation to change, greatly determines when and how most aberrant behaviors are displayed.

While the above discussion defines the interpersonal perspective relative to psychopathology, such clarification is moot if you accept that most aberrant behavior is not psychopathology. Most presenting problems seen by psychotherapists simply reflect an inadequate attempt to adjust to or cope with current environmental parameters. We should not confuse high profile, yet low base rate, diseases (schizophrenia at one percent of the population, see Gottesman, 1991) with the mundane, but ubiquitous, day-to-day problems brought about by poor parenting, stress, and normal developmental changes.

This notion of aberrant behavior reflecting adjustment not pathology is not new (see, e.g., Szasz, 1961), nor unique to the adherents of the this approach. For example, Torrey (1974), a former research psychiatrist with NIMH, argues that most problems ($\approx$75 percent) brought to mental health workers are general problems of living and another five percent involve trauma or disease to the brain (e.g., genetics, drugs, viral infections), with the remaining 20 percent somewhere in the middle. Most adherents to the systems approach would put the problem-of-living percentage close to 90 percent, with the remainder split between brain trauma and unknown.

Taking this position to its next logical step implies that psychiatric diagnoses are not only irrelevant, but potentially dangerous to the personal freedoms of the individuals involved (Szasz, 1970, 1983). This position *does not* imply that the aberrant behaviors which define the diagnostic label do not exist. It simply suggests that aberrant behavior is typically not a result of some flaw within the individual. Rather, it implies that the offending behavior reflects the individual's response to the contextual circumstances.

These aberrant behaviors are simultaneously functional and dysfunctional. At the societal level, they are dysfunctional in that the individual is perceived as flawed or sick. On the other hand, the behavior is functional in that it signals the system's inability to maintain an environment adequate for individual development and maturation. Within the system, for example, there might be alcohol or physical abuse (Griffin & Morgan, 1988), marital conflict (Hops, Sherman, & Biglan, 1990), or severe economic stress (Patterson & Forgatch, 1990). Note that severe economic stress is not the same as lack of money, but rather it refers to the behaviors associated with the concern for not having enough money. These behaviors might include increased arguing, short tempers, or social withdrawal. The specific behavior is less important than the therapist's ability to grasp the idea that such low-level behaviors can produce aberrant behavior in other family members.

More specifically to the aims of this book, "Are diagnoses pertinent to family therapists?" Yes and no. Yes, if you want to be perceived as competent at weekly clinic staffings, or if you need services reimbursed through the insurance carrier. Otherwise, traditional diagnosis of the individual (aside from the 10 percent in the speculated "other" category) is completely incompatible with the idea of a presenting problem representing a dysfunctional system.

Beware of any family therapist discussing an individual's behavior using DSM labels. These pejorative yet convenient terms for inconvenient behavior (e.g., ADHD [Attention Deficit Hyperactive Disorder]; oppositional-defiant child) imply an individual deficit (see, e.g., McGuinness, 1989, for a critical review of ADHD). This therapist is straddling a very wide, potentially disabling fence.

Role of Medication

The role and use of medication vary widely among family therapists, usually being divided along the lines of M.D. vs non-M.D. Not surprisingly, psychiatrists and family physicians who practice family therapy are more likely to value the use of medication than their non-physician colleagues. For example, some therapists think that minor dosages of medication for anxiety attacks or depression (individual deficit traits) facilitate family therapy, especially during crisis periods. Generally, however, most family therapists, despite differences in training, de-emphasize medication. Such hesitancy is theoretically consistent with the position that the individual does not process the problem, but merely expresses it. As such, medicating the individual who is expressing the symptom is analogous to beheading the messenger.

Family therapists are often asked to medicate children, typically because the behavior is a nuisance to the parents (or teachers). Unfortunately, persistent parents usually find someone who will medicate the child, despite very weak or nonexistent empirical findings supporting the use or effectiveness of the medication in removing the disorder. Consider the example of ADHD. Allusion to some vague entity like, for example, a *chemical imbalance in the brain* is usually cited as justification for the medication. Although current pharmacological treatments for some childhood disorders do *temporarily* suppress, but not remove, the offending disorder (e.g., ADHD [4–6 hrs] with Ritalin) in *some* children, it is not without a cost to the child (see Whalen & Henker, 1991). Aside from the documented physiological side effects (e.g., involuntary tics, cardiovascular changes, sleep difficulties, and possible growth suppression; see Dewan & Koss, 1989; Scarnati, 1986), there is increasing evidence that children who have been medicated for some time come to believe that the medication, not their own efforts, determines task outcomes (Whalen, Henker, Hinshaw, Heller, & Huber-Dressler, 1991). As such, it is not surprising that these pharmacological approaches have no demonstrated long-term effect on improving academic achievement or peer status (Whalen & Henker, 1991), two key traits associated with normal adolescent adjustment. Nor is it often acknowledged that many of these children come from homes characterized by parental and family dysfunction (Befera & Barkley, 1985).

In addition to the obvious ethical issues raised by medicating these children, the family therapist has several other reasons not to encourage or support medication unless it is absolutely necessary. Consistent with the theoretical model, two interrelated issues raise questions about the utility of medication in treatment. They are: (1) Why reduce the behavior that has reinforcing value within the system, until its relevancy can be determined? (2) Do pharmacologically induced behavioral changes restrict the therapist's chances of reading the relevant interactions that initially supported the behavior, and that are needed to develop effective treatment strategies?

Length of Treatment

Although it varies by orientation, family therapy is, in general, of short duration, 10 to 20 sessions (Gurman, Kniskern, & Pinsof, 1986). Multigenerational models tend to be longer than the ahistorical models. Some multigenerational models (e.g., Bowenian) stagger treatment over months, resulting in long periods of treatment (1–2 years), but only an average number of sessions; a similar strategy is used by the Milan group, but for different theoretical reasons (see chapter IV: Family Therapy Orientations).

A more volatile issue across models is not treatment length in itself, but how long treatment needs to be to insure a permanent change. All individual deficit models attempt to restructure or repair the deficit; thus, therapy is assumed to be a long-term task. Some multigenerational models, particularly object relations, advocate a similar, though more moderate position. Conversely, the ahistorical process models (e.g., structural, strategic) advocate simply changing the presenting problem, along with the initial patterns that produced the presenting problem. Treatment averages 5–15 sessions, and change in overt behavior is sufficient to terminate therapy.

The rift between the models occurs because the short-term therapy advocates assume that pattern changes will reverberate throughout the general dysfunctional system, and the system will settle down in a correct, or at least better organized, structure. Conversely, the object-relations school and individual deficit model, haunted by the specter of symptom substitution, assume that therapy should be sufficiently comprehensive (i.e., long term) to repair the deficit. Moreover, this group views short-term therapy as merely a quick fix, too brief to alter the true, core deficit.

While the theoretical merits of both positions have filled the pages of journals for years, only recently have the insurance companies stepped in on the side of the short-term approach. It seems that without empirical evidence for the superiority of long-term approaches, and with the evidence that short-term approaches are at least as effective and less costly, third-party providers are increasingly restricting length of treatment. Those who write the insurance policies have little regard for the sanctity of these theoretical positions, and probably assume, based on current information, that the only documented benefit attributable to long-term therapy is financial gain by the therapist.

WHAT FAMILY THERAPY IS NOT

As the visibility of family therapy increased in the past decade, many trendy forms of psychotherapy or pop psychology have associated themselves with family therapy. Unfortunately, they tend to be highly visible and profitable because they provide simple answers to complex problems. For most, simplicity is achieved by advocating behavioral nonresponsibility (see Disease Models below). Despite their professed connection to family therapy, they have very little in common with family therapy proper as described in this book. Most of these pseudo family-therapy models can be organized around three dimensions: Disease, Special Interest, and Converted.

Disease Models: These have the highest visibility, get the most television time, and generate the most revenue for the proponents. These include, but are not restricted to, the concepts of Shame, Inner Child, Codependency and generic Addictions (food, sex, TV, Dominoes, etc.). While these form the current victimization trend, one can be certain that new ones are on the horizon. Within this group, common themes include: *I cannot be held responsible for my behavior* (I'm addicted), *my early experiences made me like this* (don't expect much), or *I've lost myself as a person because of my relationships with others* (I can't be responsible for making stupid decisions). Irrespective of theme, the condition is assumed to be a disease, if not of the body, then of the mind. And as such, actions are beyond control (see Peele, 1989, for a scholarly assessment of this movement). This is not family therapy.

A second group associating themselves to family therapy are the *Special Interest Groups*. Their link to family therapy is unclear, yet their advertisements indicate some connection to families, or that being a member of their group somehow improves family relationships. These include, for example, men's groups, women's groups, or even groups for the vertically impaired (short people). With such diversity of potential topics, any combination is possible. Imagine a group for short people with long toes. I suppose their meetings would consist of joint commiseration about the difficulty and emotional trauma incurred when buying shoes (see Pittman, 1992, or Kaminer, 1992, for a humorous and insightful assessment of this movement). This is not family therapy.

The third and probably most controversial clustering of non-family therapy groups are those *Converted* from individual psychotherapy. These models postulate premises that are diametrical to the fundamental tenets of the interpersonal model. Yet, by adding a few family members to the session, these models assume family therapy is being done. The most visible are Transactional Analysis (Erskine, 1991), Gestalt

(Kempler, 1991), Primal Scream, Child therapy, Person-centered Family therapy (Thayer, 1991), Projective Storytelling, and Family Art Therapy (Riley, 1992). These, like the categories mentioned above, are not family therapy (see Montalvo & Haley, 1973).

3

THEORY AND TECHNIQUE

ROLE AND RELEVANCE OF THEORY

Theory determines technique. Without a grasp of the theory, therapy is mostly hand waving interspersed with techniques. Typically, such therapy lacks consistent internal logic and results in techniques that are unconnected and sometimes contradictory. Such therapy regularly achieves a high failure rate.

Theory as used in this chapter refers to a general conceptualization of how to think about family functioning and change. This book promotes a general, almost generic, idea of family dysfunction and family therapy. As noted elsewhere, it represents a composite of the ahistorical process models in family therapy, and is easy to understand for someone learning the interactional approach. These ahistorical approaches are the most frequently taught in family therapy graduate programs, and the most frequently discussed in the family therapy literature. But more importantly, they represent the truest implementation of General Systems ideas to psychotherapy. Of course, whether true implementation is necessarily better has not been decided, nor will it be in the near future. While the other orientations, Historical and Experiential, share many basic concepts with the Ahistorical Process models, they also have numerous differences. These commonalities and differences are detailed in chapter IV: *Family Therapy Orientations*.

PRESENTING PROBLEM: FUNCTION

Initial contact with the family occurs because of the presenting problem. Assuming the presenting problem reflects some interactional dysfunction, you further assume either that (1) it serves a function within the context where it occurs, or that (2) the family or individual is having difficulty adjusting to some novel experience or situation, and that the difficulty is indicated by the presenting problem. Of these two possible assumptions, the former is usually associated with long-standing problems, while the latter is most plausible around crises or reactive situations, where the reactive problem can become long term if corrective steps are not implemented in the family. All interventions are designed to *allow* the behavior to change by providing alternative behavior patterns or a new perspective on the existing pattern.

If the problem is long-standing, assume that it has a purpose relative to the (1) parents' current marital or relationship situation and quality, or (2) the developmental stage of the child or family, or (3) to some other undetermined environmental factors (e.g., teacher conflict). And possibly all three are occurring simultaneously. For example, suppose the child does not get along with the teacher, a situation that would normally be handled well by the parents. However, because of Father's recent job transfer and Mother's new job, both are spending less time with the child. Seemingly neglected, the child acts out, forcing an initial negative response by Mother and Father. Daily hassles with the child have a low-grade detrimental effect on the marital relationship. Yet, this attention for acting out is reinforcing to the child and, thus, the child's behavior is perpetuated. In this constructed scenario, the acting out functions as a means of securing attention because of problems with a teacher. The magnitude of the acting out behavior reflects the level necessary in order to get attention.

Similarly, to perpetuate a dysfunctional system, the symptom allows some member of the system (other than the IP) not to fulfill normal expectations. To illustrate, consider the father who cannot maintain a job because the son's fighting forces the family to move from one school district to another so that the father has to quit his job every few months. Yet, on questioning it becomes apparent that father has never been able to hold a job for greater than six months, and that his encouragement for the son to "stand up for himself" ensures continued fighting at school.

PRESENTING PROBLEM: CONSEQUENCES

Simply put, you need to determine, "What occurs as a result of the presenting problem?" At first glance, this question appears simple, yet it encompasses the entire range of behavioral and affective responses that surround the behavior. Specifically, theory dictates that the following areas be either directly or indirectly addressed:

- Does the presenting problem change the likelihood of any other behavior (e.g., does Mom or Dad have to get off from work)?
- Does the presenting problem increase interaction with parent(s)?
- Does the presenting problem incite antagonism with a one-to-one ratio (high degree of reciprocity; tit for tat) with the parents, or is the pattern more complex?
- What is the temporal proximity between child action and other (e.g., parent, teacher) reaction?
- Is behavior escalation necessary to get a response?
- Is the presenting problem a transformation of another, smaller problem?
- As a result of the presenting problem what does not occur?
    Who does not get to spend time with whom?
    What work is avoided?
    Who does not fight?

THEORY PROVIDES PERSPECTIVE

Theory determines, at every step, what is relevant and what is irrelevant. In effect, theory filters streams of information, and allows the therapist to attend to only those aspects of interaction that are pertinent to altering patterns.

This filtering process guides the construction of internal questions that the therapist must address when seeing a family, especially during the initial phase of therapy. These questions form an internal monologue that, in general, shapes the therapy process, and continuously changes as information accumulates. Internal process questions tend to cluster around four dimensions: impetus, definitions, the presenting problem, and change mechanisms. Below is a listing of the questions by dimensions.

Impetus

- What is *gained* by the presenting problem(s)?
- Who gains by the presenting problem(s)?
- Why does it occur *now*?
- What is its function relative to family patterns or structure?
- How does it maintain the existing pattern?
- What are the consequences of the presenting problem(s)?

Behavior Definition

- How is the presenting problem defined?

    By actual behavior
    By family committee
    By family myth

- Who reinforces or confirms the definition?

    Other families with similar problems
    TV talk shows; media; self-help books
    The use of medications
    Other mental health workers

From Behavior to Presenting Problem

- What makes the behavior a problem
  - Is it the behavior?
  - Is it the timing?
  - Is it the consequences?
- For whom is it a problem
  - Other family members?
  - School or neighborhood?

Change

- What patterns need to be altered?
- Who needs to be present?
- What is the temporal point of intervention?
  - Moment to moment
    - Immediate responses
  - Extended period
    - Days, weeks
- What structural changes need to be altered?
  - Combining sub-units
    - Joining mother and father
    - Joining siblings
    - Joining child with peers
  - Dividing units into sub-units
    - Separate parent and child
    - Form therapist coalition with each
  - Points of therapeutic leverage in the family
    - Does the IP view the behavior as a problem?
    - Do all parties view the behavior as a problem?
    - Who gains by not viewing the behavior as a problem?
    - Who is most invested in change?
    - Who is least invested in change?
    - What happens if change does not occur?
    - Who can be the best ally for the therapist?

Remember these are internal questions, the family or its

members are asked only one of these if you need confirmation, or as a therapeutic maneuver. In general, answers are obtained by general process questions (see chapter VII: *Questions*) and by observations of the family interaction.

TECHNIQUE

Theory determines technique. Techniques are therapeutic maneuvers that implement the theory at a behavioral, cognitive, or affective level. These therapeutic maneuvers (e.g., reframe) are typically associated with one or several schools of therapy. Theoretically, any subsequent reduction in the presenting problem following the use of a technique implies indirect support for the theory.

Techniques in family therapy also serve as diagnostic tools. More specifically, as each technique is implemented, either in or out of session, the response by the family provides information about relevant interactional patterns. For example, an enactment of family processes used to handle the presenting problem in the early stages of Structural family therapy provides the therapist with information about the pattern of interaction around the presenting problem, and it provides the therapist with an opportunity to explicitly question the utility of existing family responses during the interaction. This questioning, in turn, casts doubt on the current family strategy of handling the situation, thus providing the therapist with leverage to provide an alternative pattern.

Techniques have two major functions in family therapy: (1) to identify interaction patterns and structures in the family; and (2) to change these patterns and structures. These functions are interconnected; identifying patterns may, in some families, instigate changes in the pattern.

Identify Interaction Patterns and Assess Family Structure

All techniques generate data for the therapist. Each technique should provide a slightly different perspective of the same recurring pattern in the family or in the individual's contextual framework. Techniques also allow the therapist to probe the pattern and to determine a sense of structure as information is collected from the family.

Gathering information about patterns

Techniques such as enactment, or having the couple talk to each other, or having the mother negotiate with the child, or even removing a family member from the session generate relevant information about the system. Each requires in-session interaction, either between family members, or between an individual and the contextual framework influencing the dysfunctional pattern. As these interactions occur, the following questions should be addressed internally by the therapist (note—internal addressing means watch, but don't say anything):

- What was the sequence?
- How did it begin?
- Who was involved in the sequence?
- Who was not involved in the sequence?
- What was the response by each member?
- Was the response overt or covert?
- How did it end?

These questions focus on moment-to-moment behavioral sequences, but unfortunately only a partial picture of the overall situation is obtained in the session. Although you should assume that the in-session behavior is isomorphic to larger, extended out-of-session patterns, to obtain additional information ask the generic, "Describe what happens when (presenting problem) occurs." How the family responds to this question is, itself, patterned. Since the response is a construction based on a combination of client expectation, social desirability, belief systems, current anger level, and a host of other influences, *what is* said in the answer is less important than *how* they answer. Notice, for example:

- Who answers and in what order (e.g., mother, father, child)?
- How do they answer (e.g., meekly, forcefully, with pride)?
- What nonverbals are used (paralinguistic, pitch, tone, eye gaze)?

This information is tracked and maintained in mental storage by the therapist. Each separate bit of data is meaningless, but when you get sequence redundancy, hypothesize that the pattern is meaningful.

The above section deals with in-session responses, yet some techniques, especially strategic tasks, generate out-of-session responses. Thus, instead of focusing exclusively on patterns around the presenting problem, the therapist also focuses on patterns around the required task. Specifically, what sequences occurred that allowed the task to be completed, partially completed, or not completed? And further, what in-session patterns were generated by the family or individual when discussing whether or not the task was completed as assigned.

Now the therapist is observing patterns on at least two levels, patterns around the presenting problems and patterns around the response to techniques. Response to technique determines the next therapeutic move because, in family therapy, response to technique is response to treatment.

Determining Structure

Working with families is easier if you make a distinction between pattern and structure. While structure determines pattern, pattern refers to sequences of behaviors, whereas structure is the arrangement of roles and responsibilities within a family. In the case of an individual, structure refers to the arrangement of roles and responsibilities within the context of his or her life. Stated differently, structure is role behavior in response to beliefs. You can study structure two ways; either by *observing* how roles and responsibilities are manifest behaviorally, or by *asking* directly or indirectly what the client's role is in the context of the presenting problem.

Family therapy techniques generate opportunities to examine

structure. You can infer structure by taking pattern information and attaching roles to the behavior. In other words, watch what happens, then attach a role to the behavior. Assume that the behavior occurred because the role required it to occur in that particular manner, given the relevant features of the context. You are layering, one on the other, behavior and roles. In other words, behavior is prescribed by the role the individual has adopted within the system. If, for example, the father consistently looks at the mother to correct the behavior of a young child during the session, assume that the father's role is to supervise parenting, from a distance. If the mother complies and corrects the child's behavior, you can further assume that her role is to keep the child's behavior respectable in public. From these observations, you do not need to ask about their respective roles. Just assume they exist as exhibited, and do therapy accordingly.

This layering permits you to better understand the dynamics surrounding the dysfunctional behavior. In turn, you are able to anticipate responses to various techniques and better *predict* subsequent behavior. This leads to more powerful therapy because you will be more selective in the techniques that you use and avoid what would have been unsuccessful interventions.

It should be obvious that pattern and structure are interdependent. The distinction between the two provides the therapist additional breadth of perspective. Use the following four axioms as aids in distinguishing pattern and structure:

1. Structure determines the pattern
2. Pattern reflects structure
3. See the pattern and assume the structure
4. Structure is the scaffolding, and pattern is the skin

Changing Interaction Patterns

Other than assessing information, techniques also create change. In fact, most family therapy techniques are intended to change the patterns generating the presenting problem.

Techniques provide the point of entry into dysfunctional patterns. This point of entry is usually behavioral, especially if a task is assigned to change pattern. If, on the other hand, the point of entry is cognitive (e.g., myths, beliefs), then techniques usually address structure. If the theory dictates changing pattern (e.g., Strategic), you assume structure will follow. Conversely, if you seek to change structure (e.g., Structural), you assume pattern will follow.

THE ROLE OF PARENTS

Hierarchy

Across all major theoretical models, the parental unit is considered the primary source of control and influence of their children. This has two major implications. First, if the parents lack the willingness to assume control or if the parents provide poor models for behavior, then the child can be expected to show adjustment problems. Second, therapeutic attempts to alter the child's behavior always include, and typically begin with, the parents. Each of the major schools of family therapy addresses these implications in a slightly different way. A sampling is given below:

Structural has very explicit roles for the parents. They are at the top of the hierarchy and should form a bounded subsystem. Interventions involve moving the parents to the top of the hierarchy, solidifying the subsystem boundary, and altering interactions between the parental subsystem and the children (Minuchin, 1974; Minuchin & Fishman, 1981).

Strategic is similar to Structural, but with additional emphasis on power. According to this model, parents should exercise appropriate power over the children (Haley, 1980; 1987). Appropriate power is derived from parents assuming a position at the top of the hierarchy.

Behavioral places greater emphasis on parental skills. It assumes that the child's behavior reflects poor parenting, either because of skills deficit or because of some external factor impeding the expression of the skills (Belsky & Pensky, 1988; Emery, 1982; Furstenberg & Seltzer, 1986; Patterson, Reid, & Dishion, 1992; Rutter, 1983).

Multigenerational assumes that parents fail to adequately parent or lack sufficient maturity to parent, because of unresolved issues with the previous generation. These residuals create marital conflict, and the child exhibits aberrant behavior because he or she is triangled into the conflict (Boszormenyi-Nagy, 1987; Bowen, 1978).

Parental Configuration

Parental unit refers to the adults who are supposed to be in charge of the child's welfare. This can be any combination of single or married, biological or stepparents, grandparents, relatives, or adoptive parents. In reality, it does not matter if the couple is married, biological, or even custodial; if the parent is single, it does not matter if that individual is the biological parent or some relative.

Given the diversity of contemporary families, any statements about proper functioning and arrangement must be general enough to be inclusive, yet specific enough to provide guidelines for intervention. Across theoretical schools, there are several common features that the therapist should attend to in therapy. These are detailed below. For purposes of illustration, I use a married couple and a single parent.

Married or unmarried couples

UNIFIED FRONT: All rules given to the child must be consistent across both partners. Any deviation from a unified front will be exploited by the children. If a solid front is not presented on issues of discipline, privileges, and correct behavior, children will manipulate the situation to their advantage. As part of the maturation process, all children test boundaries—a perfectly noble occupation for any healthy child. If, however, the parental unit disagrees on things like correct behavior, the child will wedge himself or herself between the couple in an effort to maximize the likelihood of moving the established boundaries.

As a therapist, you should look for either overt disagreement by the parents or one parent reneging on the previously agreed-on position without conferring with the partner. Parents who disagree in front of the child will usually disagree in front of the therapist. The inability to reach or maintain a parenting agreement may signal poor marital quality.

CONFLICT LEVEL : One particularly good way to produce acting-out behavior in children is to have marital conflict (Emery, 1982; Grych & Fincham, 1990). Depending on the theoretical model, some theorists immediately assume that marital conflict accompanies problem behaviors in the child (Framo, 1982), whereas others maintain a wait and see attitude (Colapinto, 1991).

Single Parent

Parental responsibility

Unfortunately, a consequence of being a single parent is loneliness. And as a result, a common situation among single parents with acting-out kids is that the parent has abdicated the parenting role for a friendship role with the child. This friendship will often force the parent to act in the best interest of maintaining the friendship rather than doing what is best for the child. Without the necessary consistency of good parenting, the child is more likely to test boundaries and eventually develop behavioral problems.

Environmental support

A second problem that typically occurs with the abdication of parental authority is the general lack of environmental support. This can take the form of sparse monetary support (i.e., failure to receive child support), no child care support either at home or the job site, inadequate income, no time out from the child, few confidants, and general stress without relief (see Wahler & Dumas, 1989). All affect parenting skill and tolerance, and make it much easier to use the child as a friend, despite the long term consequences.

These problems are often compounded by the relationship with the ex-spouse. Continued fighting with the ex-spouse is associated with adjustment problems in the child (Amato & Keith, 1991). Or the child may use the hostile relationship for leverage to get favors from either the custodial or noncustodial parent, and lack of discipline emerges as a consequence. Another common scenario is that the acting out child forces the ex-spouses to stop fighting and form a shaky alliance in an effort to stop the presenting problem. These alliances typically do little good and provide fertile ground for one spouse blaming the other for the child's problem.

ROLE OF THE THERAPIST

Art or Science

No discussion of theory and technique is complete without considering the role of the therapist. Theory dictates how the therapist thinks; technique is what the therapist does in response to the thinking. Although most schools of family therapy have written about the role of the therapist, that role always seems secondary to the flashy cure (see Chapter V: *The Therapist*). Unfortunately, it seems that fanatical adherence to techniques, combined with the vagueness of supposedly ideal therapists skills (e.g., Truax & Carkhuff, 1967), produces therapists who may be technically correct, yet generally ineffective. They might, for example, know how to sit to express positive regard. Most can move chairs. A few can even produce paradoxes with ease. But of course, when delivered merely as a technique, most of these acts are done at the wrong time, without rationale, and, not surprisingly, with little client benefit.

Theory, not technique, should determine the behavior of the therapist. Adopting this perspective, techniques are not viewed as a set of behavioral acts independent of context, but rather as behavioral extensions of the theory. Effective therapeutic acts (i.e., techniques) evolve during therapy as a way of thinking, not as solitary acts. As such, all therapeutic interaction should be considered therapy, yet when we describe therapy we tend to focus only on the overt, the redundant, and the flashy. Stated differently, every nuance of every act or statement that occurs in therapy should be directed by theory. These small nuances establish the foundation that allow the effective implementation of the larger, more overt technical acts often associated with wizardry.

WIZARDRY REQUIRES PREPARATION

Books on therapy seem to imply that any individual, after having read an ample number of books or attended at least 3.5 workshops, will be a good therapist. In effect, there is the assumption that therapeutic skill accumulates at some rate proportional to exposure to knowledge about the skill. This is an unrealistic expectation. It implies, analogously, that you should be able to run faster as a function of how many 100 meter races you attend or, even better, how many coaching clinics you attend. What is even worse is that this expectation ignores individual differences and disregards the therapist as artisan. As the sculptor shapes clay, the good therapist molds an asymmetrical social interaction; it is asymmetrical because the therapist is directing what occurs during the interaction.

The ability to direct social interaction comes from two sources: the inherent social skills of the therapist, and the ability to translate theory into behavior. The former is probably not teachable, and the latter, although teachable, depends on clarity of thinking as it pertains to the theory. Just as a painter anticipates how the finished painting should look, depending on brush stroke and color density, the therapist should anticipate how the family will respond to subtle therapeutic maneuvers.

SUMMARY

Theory determines technique. Techniques produce responses in the client that determine how the therapist perceives the family structure. Stated differently, the response you get from a client depends on the technique used to elicit the information. And we use techniques that generate responses that confirm the theory. Hence, it is easy to understand why everyone thinks that his or her theory is correct.

Techniques express the theory. As extensions of the theory, they provide the conceptual lens for gathering information about system patterns and structure. Theory also determines every aspect of therapist behavior. For example, it determines what questions are asked, how the questions are asked, and what to focus on in therapy. Theory dictates therapist moment-to-moment behavior and the ordering of intervention moves and techniques.

4

FAMILY THERAPY ORIENTATIONS

Family therapy orientations can be roughly divided into three broad categories based on their points of reference in therapy: Ahistorical Process, Historical, and Experiential (Levant, 1984). All agree that families are comprised of interlocking subunits that influence the presenting problem yet, each works from different theoretical premises about how best to remove the presenting problem. Each broad area is briefly described below. Within each orientation, several representative models are outlined. Because of space constraints, each outline will contain only a synopsis of the general premises and terms associated with each model. These outlines provide exposure to the models; extensive references provide the reader with suggested readings.

AHISTORICAL PROCESS

Unifying Features

The Ahistorical Process orientation attempts to remove the presenting problem by altering family interaction patterns.

Advocates of this position assume that current interaction processes may or may not be related to the etiology of the presenting problem, but certainly contribute to its maintenance. In general, the goal of therapy is to remove the presenting problem. Levant (1984; see his Structure/Process) identifies four characteristics of the Ahistorical Process orientation:

1. Ahistorical: present oriented; history of the presenting problem is all that is needed
2. Behavioral: focus on overt behaviors; recent emphasis on attribution and belief system as a handle to manipulate behavior
3. Interactional: attempts to alter interactional patterns; assumes that relevant individuals in the immediate environment reciprocally determine behavior
4. Active therapist: active and directive in session; assumes compliance and change

Within the Ahistorical Process orientation, it is possible to divide the orientation into four models: Communication, Structural, Behavioral, and Psychoeducational. Although not arbitrary, this four-part division is somewhat heuristic because of the extensive theoretical overlap among the models in this orientation. But because of some historical and technique differences, this division helps the family therapy newcomer grasp these subtle distinctions.

Communication Model (MRI, Strategic, Milan)

The Communication model is not a single therapy model, rather it includes several similar models that share a core of common characteristics. Therapy within the Communication model emphasizes general systems/cybernetic thinking, requires a detailed analysis of the presenting problem, identifies specific behavior patterns that are associated with the presenting problem, and advocates altering relevant interaction sequences.

MRI

The Mental Research Institute (MRI) in Palo Alto, California began operating in the late 1950s as a research project to study schizophrenics and their families. This project was headed by Don Jackson, and had Jules Riskin and Virginia Satir on the staff. Simultaneously, Gregory Bateson and his research team (Jay Haley, John Weakland, William Fry) were studying communication patterns in schizophrenic families in Palo Alto. During this period, there was considerable cross fertilization of ideas and concepts. When the money ran out on the Bateson project, Weakland, Haley, and Fry joined Satir and Jackson at MRI. At about the same time (1961), Paul Watzlawick also joined the staff at MRI. As the staff changed (Satir to the Esalen Institute in Big Sur, California in 1966, and Haley to the Philadelphia Child Guidance Clinic in 1967), other family therapy luminaries joined the staff over time—Richard Fisch, Arthur Bodin, Carlos Sluzki. During the early years, several influencing theories laid the foundation for the tenets of MRI; they were:

- General Systems Theory (von Bertalanffy, 1933; 1950; 1966; 1968; 1976; 1981)
- Cybernetics (Ashby, 1956; Wiener, 1961)
- Don Jackson's own writings (Jackson, 1960; 1964; see, also Greenberg, 1977, and Watzlawick, Beavin, & Jackson, 1967)
- Milton Erickson's indirect hypnosis techniques via Haley (Haley, 1963; 1973)
- Gregory Bateson (Bateson, 1972; 1979; Bateson, Jackson, Haley, & Weakland, 1956)

Contemporary positions within this model are clearly forwarded in two books, *Change: Principles of Problem Formation and Problem Resolution* (Watzlawick, Weakland, & Fisch, 1974) and *The Tactics of Change* (Fisch, Weakland, & Segal, 1982) and a chapter (Segal, 1991).

General assumptions

- Definition of a system: "Two or more communicants in the process of or at the level of defining the nature of their relationship" (Watzlawick et al., 1967, p. 121)
- Circular causality: behavior is simultaneously cause and effect
- Equifinality: different beginnings or circumstances may produce similar outcomes; we cannot assume the input based on output
- Equipotentiality: similar beginnings may produce different outcomes; we cannot assume that similar events across individuals will have similar effects
- Wholeness and non-summativity: the system is whole in and of itself, and cannot be viewed as the sum of its parts
- Views of communication
    A person cannot not communicate (Watzlawick et al., 1967)
    Every communication has a content and a relationship aspect such that the latter classifies the former (Watzlawick et al., 1967)
    The communicant's punctuation of the interaction determines the nature of a relationship
- Correct behavior: There is not necessarily a right or wrong way that an individual or family should behave; assumes a non-normative position about families. MRI does not intervene in an area unless an individual has a complaint or a family member has a complaint about the problem (Fisch et al., 1982).
- Reality: holds a Constructivist position; they talk about views, and suggest that it is inappropriate to discuss reality (Watzlawick, 1984); they maintain that, "All purposeful human behavior depends greatly on the views or premises people hold, which govern their interpretations of situations, events, and relationships" (Fisch et al., 1982, p. 5)
- Resolution of the presenting problem is the goal of therapy
- The presenting problem represents what the client wants to

remove, and should be used as an index of change (Bodin, 1981)

- All behavior, good or bad, is shaped and maintained by the system in which it occurs. Behavior is reinforced by social interactions in the immediate environment.

Assessment and treatment

- Change

    First-order change: change that occurs within a system, yet the system itself remains unchanged (Watzlawick et al., 1974). Change that does not force a change in the structure of the larger system. In many situations, first-order change is sufficient to remove the presenting problem.

    Second-order change: a change in the structure of the system forcing new rules and internal order (Watzlawick et al., 1974).

- Mishandling a problem creates a bigger problem

    Deny that there is a problem; action is needed but not taken

    Problem is either not solvable or nonexistent; unnecessary action is taken

    Attempt a first-order change when a only a second-order change will remove the problem (Bodin, 1981)

Techniques

All tasks (usually out of session) are intended to remove the presenting problem. It is assumed that the problem exists because initial attempts to fix the problem were mishandled, and as a consequence the situation has gotten worse. As such, the underlying rule of all prescriptions for change requires that the client do something different than was done before. This requires that the therapist get a detailed description of the presenting problem and what has been tried to eliminate the problem. Emphasis is on determining what interaction in the current environment maintains the displeasing behavior, and how changes in the interaction will affect the presenting problem.

Therapists using this model are quick to employ reframes in

order to get (1) a shift in client perspective and (2) compliance. Among all family therapy orientations, MRI stands above the rest with its emphasis on specific behavior change techniques. Most of the techniques were derived from Erickson (Haley, 1963; 1973), and given theoretical support through the writings of Watzlawick & colleagues (Bodin, 1981; Fisch et al., 1982; Watzlawick, 1976; 1978; Watzlawick et al., 1974). Some of the more popular techniques are:

- The Devil's Pact—creating a situation where client gives the therapist carte blanche before any action is taken
- Making overt the covert—spontaneous or uncontrollable behavior is made overt (i.e., controllable), and thereafter it can no longer be used to stall therapy progress
- Advertising rather than concealing—calling attention to physical features or behavior (physically, social) in situations where power or leverage resides in its concealment; after it is obvious (advertisement), its presence cannot be used as a reason not to take action
- Prescribe the symptom—as a means of controlling the symptom; similar to scheduling the symptom
- Replace the symptom—with another more beneficial one
- Behavior prescription—produce the behavior even when it is not present, or needed; practice removes the notion of uncontrollability
- Utilizing resistance—in situations where the individual is not responding to task, ask that he or she slow down, or better yet, not change; the client then faces the dilemma of complying with the therapist (i.e., not doing anything different) or not complying, which requires changing

Role of the therapist

- Therapeutic skills are assumed; emphasis is on the delivery of techniques

Strategic

Strategic therapy is both a type of therapy and a model of family therapy. In the first case, it refers to any therapy that is brief, problem-focused, and dependent on an active therapist (Haley, 1973; Rabkin, 1977). As a model of family therapy, Strategic therapy refers to the specific body of work created by Jay Haley (1963; 1973;1980;1984;1987). More recently, this work has been expanded by the writings of Madanes (1981;1984), Hoffman (1981), and Stanton (1981). Strategic therapy, as it evolved from Haley, reflects an amalgam of the thinking and techniques of Milton Erickson, MRI, and Structural family therapy. Having spent time with Erickson (Haley, 1973), at MRI, and with Minuchin in Philadelphia, Haley was in a unique position to integrate these perspectives into a single model of therapy. Like MRI, Strategic therapy advocates the use of behavioral techniques as the means to change family and dyadic interaction patterns. Unfortunately, this emphasis on technique often overshadows the power of the therapeutic relationship; as noted by Haley and others, it is this relationship between the individual or family and the therapist that determines the change. The task just determines how.

General assumptions

- Emphasis on hierarchy—parents should be in charge and in control
- Emphasis on power—who is in control and under what conditions does that control change (see Stanton, 1981)
- The symptom is a metaphor for the dysfunctional sequences in the system, symptoms do not reflect the individual, but rather represent what is occurring in the family (Haley, 1987); symptoms are homeostatic mechanisms that regulate family transactions
- Helplessness, incompetence, and illness provide a position of power in the family (Madanes, 1981)
- Normal family life transitions are points of greatest vulnerability; the inability to adapt to change stresses the system's rules and may produce dysfunction

- Individuals and families have psychological resources that will enable them to change; assumes that individuals or families have the ability to self-correct if provided the opportunity via therapy (Haley, 1973)
- Resistance to change is a natural by-product of stability; in therapy it should be expected, and used to facilitate change
- Developing insight in patients is unimportant to solving problems; Erickson notes that healthy functioning families are much less preoccupied with themselves and their own motivations (Haley, 1973)
- Therapy is brief in terms of number of sessions, yet if need be, new problems may dictate that additional therapy be done on each specific problem
- Families are unable to solve their problems because they are locked into a sequence of dysfunctional behaviors
- Problems in the identified patient cannot be expected to change unless the family system changes
- The triangle is the basic building block of any emotional interpersonal system; when tension between members of a two-person system becomes high, a third person is brought into the picture
- Not all elements in a sequence need to be altered; only enough to instigate change
- Treatment is successful only when there is a beneficial change in the presenting problem

Assessment and treatment

- In the initial session, the therapist establishes rapport, defines the problem, contracts to solve the problem, determines sequences supporting the problem, and assigns a task to alter the sequence
- In subsequent sessions, compliance with the previous task is assessed, and a new task is given
- System-level diagnosis is often done by the therapist's making an intervention and seeing how the system responds to it
- Attention is paid to the sequence of communication and behaviors

- Avoids diagnostic labels
- Focus in on the present; history is relevant only to the presenting problem
- Focus on process (interaction sequences) rather than on content (what is said)
- Out-of-session tasks are given
- The therapist works to substitute new behavior patterns for existing dysfunctional ones
- Task compliance and noncompliance provide information about the system

Techniques

- Direct, indirect, and paradoxical directives (Haley, 1987)
- Paradoxical intention:

> *prescribing the symptom*—therapist instructs the client to engage in problem behavior
> *restraining the change*—therapist tries to deny possibility of change
> *positioning*—therapist tries to shift problematic "position" by accepting or exaggerating that position

- Reframing and positive connotations are frequently used, especially around the presenting problem and after task noncompliance
- Exaggerating the symptom
- Get the client to *pretend* to change
- Get the client to *pretend* to have the presenting problem or symptom
- Changes behaviors using ordeals (Haley, 1984)
- Straightforward directives in session (Haley, 1987)
- Uses many of the same techniques used by MRI (see Madanes, 1981; 1984)

Role of the therapist

- Therapist will alter the perception of the presenting problem in order to make it amenable to modification

- Modifies the presenting problem through intermediate goals; small changes lead to larger changes
- Therapist will use any technique as long as it might work to change behavioral sequences
- Therapist assumes responsibility for treatment progress and success
- Therapist must be aware of family value structure, cultural perspective, etc. in order to devise effective tasks
- The therapist is active and initiates what happens during treatment
- The therapist must be creative in devising tasks and directives
- Delivery is at least as important as the task itself (L'Abate, Ganahl, & Hansen, 1986)

Milan (Systemic)

The Milan approach, sometimes referred to as the Systemic approach, is similar to MRI. Like MRI, sessions are few in number, but tend to be 4–6 weeks apart. Also like MRI, therapeutic change relies on reframes (positive connotations) and tasks (i.e., rituals; see, e.g., Imber-Black, Roberts, & Whiting, 1989). In many respects, the Milan model is the truest family therapy adaptation to the systems perspective; these practitioners were influenced by Bateson's writings (1972), and the work of MRI. The primary figures in the Milan approach are Mara Selvini-Palazzoli (1988, Selvini-Palazzoli, Boscolo, Cecchin, & Prata, 1978; Selvini-Palazzoli, Cirillo, Selvini, & Sorrentino, 1989), Luigi Boscolo (Boscolo, Cecchin, Hoffman, & Penn, 1987), Guiliana Prata, and Gianfranco Cecchin from Milan, Italy; from America, the figures are Peggy Penn (1982;1985), Lynn Hoffman (1981;1988), and Karl Tomm (1984a,b). Systemic Family Therapy attempts to alter the dysfunctional family patterns by inducing second-order change (system level) via circular questioning (Tomm, 1988), positive connotations, and behavior change task assignments (e.g., rituals, prescriptions). In the last decade, the Systemic approach has undergone several major shifts in personnel and theoretical tenets. In the personnel area,

Selvini-Palazzoli and Prata split from Boscolo and Cecchin, each forming a unique treatment and training facility. With regard to theoretical tenets, as outcomes were assessed and the model matured, the Milan approach moved from using paradoxical interventions to giving invariant prescriptions, and more recently, to variant prescriptions (tailored to the family).

General assumptions

- Assumes that symptoms serve a function within the dysfunctional family system
- Assumes that in order for the system to survive, one of the family members is sacrificed
- No specific behavioral goals are negotiated with the family; change occurs randomly as information is added to the system via questions and rituals
- Early Milan used paradoxical injunctions to alter interaction patterns
- Middle Milan used an invariant prescription (i.e., the task was the same for all families irrespective of symptom); specifically, parents record the reactions of family members who are told that the parents have a secret, and eventually parents are told to secretly disappear from the home for varying lengths of time; reactions to the "secret" and the sojourns generate information for the sessions (Selvini-Palazzoli approach)
- Recent Milan uses prescriptions that vary by family and problem (Selvini-Palazzoli approach)
- Boscolo and Cecchin emphasize the questioning process in therapy as agent that generates change

Assessment and treatment

- Treatment lasts about 10 sessions
- Sessions are scheduled about 4–6 weeks apart
- Male and female co-therapists are used; a therapy team observes
- Symptom change occurs as result of interaction changes

brought about by therapeutic rituals or prescriptions, and in-session questions

- Each session is divided into stages: first, hypotheses are generated after the family is asked circular questions, then the co-therapists meet with the team to discuss a strategy (e.g., require a ritual), the co-therapists then meet again with the family and present the task
- The main intervention is usually a ritual or positive connotation
- Rituals force the family to alter interactions that are thought (by the therapy team) to perpetuate the family myths that justify patterns associated with the symptom
- The therapy team behind the glass is used strategically: offers opinions, makes suggestions, or disagrees with the co-therapist team
- Circular questions gather information, generate hypotheses, and alter the family's perspective of the family (Tomm, 1984a,b; 1988)

Techniques

- Questions, rituals, and positive connotations seek to introduce information into the system, and thereby alter interactions
- A positive connotation (similar to a reframe in MRI) specifically reframes the symptom so that it appears to serve a possible function within the family
- The prescriptive intervention is tailored to change the rules of the family system by focusing on changing the primitive, underlying myth that regulates the system
- Circular questioning prompts interaction, which generates the information used to form hypotheses about symptom function
- A ritual directs specific family members to change their behavior under certain circumstances; usually rituals prescribe a time and place for the behavior to occur

Role of the therapist

- Therapist maintains a neutral stance, asking circular questions, and occasionally makes observations and conveys hypotheses from the therapy team
- Therapist neutrality provides the family nothing to react against

New Communication Models

Solution Focused

A variant of MRI, the Solution Focused approach, first defines the problem with great specificity, and probes for situations when the problem does not occur (O'Hanlon & Weiner-Davis, 1989). Derived from the flexible techniques advocated by Milton Erickson, the Solution Focused approach teaches individuals, couples, or families alternative ways of viewing the problem situation by seeking information about when the problem was not a problem (de Shazer, 1988). By asking questions and pointing out previous examples where the individual successfully avoided or solved the problem, the Solution Focused therapist provides a new perspective about the possibility of change.

Externalization

A recent approach that combines a little MRI, some Milan, and a touch of Solution Focused is Michael White's Externalization approach, which allows the family to view the problem as external, and thus amenable to change (White, 1986; White & Epston, 1990). It provides the family with an alternative story of the problem; this negotiated story implies that the problem does not reflect negatively on the family but is external to them, and that with concerted effort, it can be fixed. Using rhetorical questions, the therapist constructs this new story that leads the family toward a new perspective of the problem.

Structural Family Therapy

Reasonableness of techniques, ease of implementation, and theoretical clarity have made Structural Family Therapy the most popular form of family therapy. Initially developed to work with young delinquents, Structural Family Therapy attempts to change family patterns through in-session manipulation of family interaction. It assumes that dysfunctional behavior reflects an inadequate structure in the family system. For example, parents allow a child to enter the parental subsystem, possibly diffusing marital conflict while simultaneously producing a dysfunctional child. Salvador Minuchin and colleagues (Braulio Montalvo, Dick Auerswald) initially developed the premises of Structural Family Therapy at the Wiltwyck School for Boys in New York during the early 1960s (Minuchin, Montalvo, Guerney, Rosman, & Schumer, 1967). In 1965, Minuchin became the Director of the Philadelphia Child Guidance Clinic, and while he was there, other well known therapists spent time with him and Montalvo (e.g., Jay Haley, Cloe Madanes, Harry Aponte, Bernice Rosman, Charles Fishman). Therapy within this model is action-oriented, and altering the presenting problem is considered the goal of therapy. There are numerous good books and chapters that make this model accessible to the beginning family therapist (e.g., Aponte & VanDeusen, 1981; Colapinto, 1991; Minuchin, 1974; Minuchin & Fishman, 1981; Minuchin, Rosman, & Baker, 1978).

General assumptions

- The goal of therapy is to change boundaries and hierarchies sufficiently to allow the presenting problem to be unnecessary
- The major dimensions of the model are (see Aponte & VanDeusen, 1981):

  Boundaries—defines the roles necessary to carry out functions: defines who participates, and how; invisible barriers that surround individuals and subsystems, regulating the amount of contact with others

> *Alignment*—joining or opposition of one member of a system to another in carrying out an operation; subsystems are formed through alignment
>
> *Power*—relative influence of each member on the outcome of an activity; this ability is relative to the activity engaged in; is determined by the active and passive combinations of family members

- Interactions in a family derive from the internal structure; structure refers to the roles that organize all behavior that occurs to fulfill the functions of the family
- Boundaries are categorized by their level of permeability; a clear boundary indicates that individuals can permeate the subsystem at a regulated and optimal amount
- Individual, subsystem, and family boundaries can range from diffuse (allows enmeshment) to rigid (allows disengagement)

> Rigid boundaries are overly restrictive and restrain contact to outside systems, resulting in disengagement; disengaged individuals or subsystems are isolated from each other
>
> Enmeshed subsystems provide a sense of mutual support, at the expense of autonomy

- As a means of adapting to change (developmental or extrafamilial), the family develops a structure that subsequently determines all interactions; inadequate structure produces inadequate adaptation, and results in dysfunctional behavior
- In order to adequately adjust to changes (developmental or extrafamilial), the family must be flexible, and have the capacity to alter its internal structure

Assessment and treatment

- When the presenting problem has been adequately defined and the structural location of the dysfunction has been identified, the therapy will focus on that problem until it has been removed
- Small changes in interactions are accepted as progress

- Treatment emphasizes structural changes in session, although homework assignments may be given to reinforce the new patterns
- Assessment occurs through the asking of questions, the watching of interactions, and the use of enactments; the objective is to locate the structural fault and modify it

Techniques

- Joining—making the family feel comfortable; uses the behaviors, language, and communication style of the family
- Enactment—forces the family to enact interactional patterns associated with the presenting problem; this provides structural information to the therapist
- Reframing (see MRI)
- Task-setting within the family—forces new transactions with specific goals; these are intended to alter structure
- Restructuring—changing the transactions of the family by changing the structure
    - by adding or subtracting subsystems
    - by exaggerating the symptom
    - by moving to a new symptom
    - by deemphasizing the symptom
    - by relabeling the symptom
    - by creating new structures by altering interactions, or by reinforcing new patterns

Role of the therapist

- The therapist is active, responsive to the family, uses humor, and demands action in the session
- The therapist seeks to determine where in the system the structure fails to carry out its function

Behavioral

Derived from learning theory, Behavioral Family Therapy (BFT) began in the late 1950s and early 1960s as a treatment for childhood disorders (e.g., autism). Through the pioneering work of Gerald Patterson (1982), parent training as a vehicle for changing families became a legitimate form of family therapy. Although often unfairly criticized for being linear because of its emphasis on the analysis of antecedents, consequences, and contingencies of the problem behavior, it falls well within the thinking of contemporary family therapy. By definition, any analysis of antecedents and consequences must assume the potency of contextual (i.e., familial) contingencies. Moreover, most of the contemporary writings in BFT, Behavior Parent Training, and Behavioral Marital Therapy (Holtzworth-Munroe & Jacobson, 1991) are almost overly inclusive in their assessment; they see as relevant to the presenting problem anything that reinforces or extinguishes a behavior or predisposes an individual or dyad to exhibit a behavior (Bandura, 1978). This includes not only intrafamilial influencers of reinforcement (e.g., parenting skills, family belief systems, marital quality, adult dysfunction), but other possible factors such as stress, genetic predisposition, and social context (e.g., neighborhoods) (see Patterson, Reid, & Dishion, 1992).

This model assumes that behavior reflects a learned response. More specifically, the behavior exhibited by an individual at any given time reflects the complex, cumulative process of learning derived from dynamic interactions that the individual has had with his or her environment. Major figures in this area are Gerald Patterson (1971; 1982; Patterson et al., 1992), John Reid, Tom Dishion, Ian Falloon, Hyman Hops, Robert Whaler, Rex Forehand, and Robert Liberman. In the closely related area, Behavior Marital Therapy (BMT), prominent figures include Neil Jacobson (Jacobson & Margolin, 1979; Holtzworth-Munroe & Jacobson, 1991), Richard Stuart, Gayla Margolin, Donald Baucom, Norman Epstein (Baucom & Epstein, 1990), Howard Markman, and Kurt Hahlweg. A model that integrates systems and behavioral, and has good empirical support, is James Alexander's Functional Family Therapy (Alexander & Parsons, 1982; Barton & Alexander, 1981). Recommended writings include Patterson (1971; 1982), Patterson et al. (1992), Gordon and Davidson (1981), Falloon (1991), Wahler and Dumas (1989), and Holtzworth-Munroe and Jacobson (1991).

General assumptions

- A wide range of behavior is functionally related to environmental events
- Parents have power to generate change
- Interpersonal problems between parents may preclude them from working together in the collaborative set needed for united parenting
- Assumes that treatment failure typically occurs when the therapist does not provide the proper structure and behavior change techniques relevant to the family
- Family members are those individuals whose interpersonal relationship with the child provide a source of reinforcement for the child; implies that the individuals need not be related
- The concept of boundaries is implicit in behavioral family therapy
- Assumes that some children have a constitutional predisposition (i.e., temperament) toward antisocial or aggressive behavior, and that the behavior can be modified by appropriate parental skills (Falloon, 1991)
- Parents of acting out children typically negative track (i.e., only see the bad), inconsistently reinforce good behavior, and inconsistently or inappropriately use punishment
- Families of children with behavior problems typically do not have clearly defined rules about behavior and responsibility
- Families of children with behavior problems are characterized by low levels of praise, high levels of aversive interactions, and high levels of coercive processes (Patterson, 1982)
- Goals are to teach the parent skills to increase the child's repertoire of desirable behaviors, while decreasing the frequency of problem behaviors
- Family members are considered the most relevant (i.e., most powerful) deliverers of reinforcements in the child's environment

- The reduction of negative affect expression does not imply that positive affect will increase
- Reciprocity implies the equitable exchange among family members of positives or negatives; the principle of reciprocity is assumed to operate in families
- Parents can, and will, fail to implement treatment
- Dysfunctional patterns of interaction are assumed to represent the best efforts to respond to the current circumstances, given the skill level and motivation among the family members
- Marital dissatisfaction and adult psychopathology adversely influence treatment outcome
- Assessment consists of a behavioral interview, behavioral checklists, and analog and naturalistic observations
- Primary reason for nonsuccess in BFT is parental inconsistency

Assessment and treatment

- Assessment of the presenting problem

    determine response characteristics
    obtain history
    who is associated with the problem
    determine antecedents
    determine consequences
    duration
    frequency
    location

- Assessment considers the covariations that exist between subsystems; assumes that movement or change in one sub-unit affects the other sub-units
- Assessment is broadly determined in two stages:

    Problem analysis—specific definition and location of the behaviors associated with the presenting problem
    Functional analysis—during interactions with other family members, locate the relevant antecedents and

       consequences that are thought to maintain the presenting problem

- Marital quality is determined as part of the initial assessment
- Attempts are made to identify situations (e.g., who, when, where) when the presenting problems are likely and unlikely to occur; treatment is based on decreasing the likelihood of occurrence
- Parents are taught to observe, count, and record the child's behavior
- BFT is usually contracted for a limited number of sessions; this can be renegotiated as new problems emerge
- Assessment occurs throughout the treatment period to determine if, and how, relevant parent-child interactions change as a result of treatment

Techniques

- Standard techniques include:
  Time out
  Modeling
  Prompting
  Shaping
  Behavioral Rehearsal
  Education-developmental information; parenting skills
  Communication skills training
  Problem-solving skills
  Contingency Contracting—a contract outlining desired
      and undesired behaviors

Role of the therapist

- The therapist is viewed as a consultant to the parents
- Treatment is designed to fit the parent's ability to implement the desired changes
- Recent emphasis on the quality of the therapeutic relationship as a major component in the success of therapy (Patterson & Forgatch, 1985)

Psychoeducational

Within the last decade, several groups of clinicians began treating schizophrenics and their families using an education-based model. This Psychoeducational model seeks to teach the families about schizophrenia, reduce stress in family interactions, and teach strategies to reduce the chances of relapse (McFarlane, 1991). Drawing from the Expressed Emotion (EE) literature (e.g., Leff & Vaughn, 1985), these clinicians decided that it might be possible to reduce relapse rates by reducing familial stress and conflict through education about the disease and medication, along with some skills training combined with some traditional family therapy techniques (most similar to Structural). This model has received consistent empirical support for reducing relapse (Anderson, Reiss, & Hogarty, 1986). The tenets of this model are consistent with an emerging area of research that suggests that marital or family quality can modify the course and severity of many common diseases and aliments (see, e.g., Griffin & Greene, in press; Melamed & Brenner, 1990). Important individuals in this model are Carol Anderson, Douglas Reiss, Gerald Hogarty, Michael Goldstein, and Ian Falloon (Falloon, 1988;Falloon, Boyd, & McGill, 1984).

General assumptions

- Schizophrenia has a biological basis, environmental stressors are needed for symptom manifestation (Gottesman, 1991; McFarlane, 1991)
- Hostile or conflictual households associated with schizophrenia are a consequence of the disease, not a cause
- The goal is to maximize the functioning and coping abilities of patients and their families, and to prevent relapse
- Expressed Emotion (EE) (critical or intrusion remarks, or attitudes) are associated with high relapse rates; Psychoeducational techniques seek to reduce EE
- Stress exacerbates the symptoms, which leads to decompensation and relapse
- The goal is to establish a collaborative partnership with

families so that the members feel empathized with, supported, and capable of dealing with the patient

Assessment and treatment

- First stage of therapy is joining the family; non-blaming
- Second stage of therapy is education: one-day workshop on
  the disease, the importance of medication, and the detrimental effect of environmental and intra-familial stress
- Third stage of therapy is regularly scheduled family therapy sessions; these resemble Structural Family therapy, and
  focus on family dynamics for the purpose of reducing marital and family conflict and general levels of hostility (EE)
- Fourth stage of therapy is rehabilitation for the patient:
  strategies are developed that allow the patient to live and
  function at an optimal level
- Families are encouraged to provide an atmosphere of low
  stimulation and expectation, but not without structure or
  limit-setting
- Patients are not allowed to engage in strange or irritating
  behavior that upsets others in house; no drugs or violence
  in the house
- Patients are given chores and consequences for rule
  violations
- Treatment will last from one year to 18 months; long enough
  to modify the likelihood of a relapse

Techniques

- Education about the disease and medication
- Skills building: social & communication skills, stress
  reduction
- Structural Family therapy techniques

Role of the therapist

- The therapist has a multipurpose role: teacher, therapist,
  consultant, and liaison to the medical field

HISTORICAL

Unifying Features

Although diverse in technique, the Historical orientation has several common characteristics: (1) each model has psychoanalytic roots, (2) individual growth and the process of individuation within the family are important, (3) therapy tends to be longer, and (4) the therapist tends to be more passive in the session than either of the other two orientations. These sweeping generalizations are simplistic, yet capture the theory, the goal of therapy, and therapist behavior. Historical models, despite their proponents' proclamations to the contrary (see, e.g., Nichols, 1987), have become less popular in family therapy during the last decade.

This drop in popularity comes from several directions. First, many of the founding fathers of family therapy were traditionally trained psychoanalytical psychiatrists—a background no longer representative of the typical practitioner of family therapy. Second, as a group, the Historical models have consistently failed to produce, nor have they even attempted to produce, empirical evidence of effectiveness (Gurman, Kniskern, & Pinsof, 1986), as have the behavioral and briefer therapies. Third, and specific to the Object Relations model, several of the fundamental premises about infant and child development have not held up under academic scrutiny. In particular, Stern (1985) and other child developmentalists call into question the nice, orderly progression of individualization that infants are supposed to go through, at least according to Object Relations theory. Similarly, the Object Relations model utilizes concepts drawn from Attachment Theory (Bowlby, 1969; 1973) which, in recent years, has had its supporting literature severely criticized for its methodological weaknesses (see, e.g., Lamb, Thompson, Gardner, Charnov, & Estes, 1984; Lamb, Thompson, Gardner, & Charnov, 1985).

Nonetheless, the Historical orientation is one of the primary approaches in family therapy and, in fact, the area has recently begun to integrate more systems thinking into its traditional psychoanalytic thought (e.g., Kirschner & Kirschner, 1986).

Object Relations

Object Relations family therapy is the principle psychoanalytic model used to treat families. The primary goal in Object Relations family therapy is to have parents work through how each projects onto the other family members images based on past (usually during the infant period) relationships. More specifically, the theory suggest that we internalize (introject) objects in the environment that both please and frustrate us as infants; the initial, and most prominent, object is the mother. Through fantasy, reality is distorted so that the infant is able to hold these seemingly incompatible (frustration/pleasure) positions simultaneously. Over time, images or representations of these interactions are internalized, and the internalized objects (introjects) form the basis for how individuals form and evaluate all subsequent close relationships.

Specific to family therapy, the founding fathers of the psychoanalytic movement were Christian Midelfort, Theodore Lidz (Lidz, Cornelison, & Fleck, 1965), Lyman Wynne, and Nathan Ackerman (1958; 1966). In fact, Ackerman was one of the primary leaders in the family therapy field during the 1950s and 1960s. Other major figures concerned with early Object Relations theory development were Melanie Kein (1948), Margaret Mahler (Mahler, Pine, & Bergman, 1975), and Otto Kernberg (1976). Recently, Kirschner and Kirschner (1986) and Scharff and Scharff (1987) have attempted to combine the systems and psychodynamic orientations into a singular model.

General assumptions

- Individuals form introjects (internalized objects) based on previous relationships that determine how current relationships are enacted
- Therapy involves working through, or becoming aware of,

unconscious patterns from early childhood that affect current relationships, including the therapeutic relationship
- Defense mechanisms range from the mature (e.g., Altruism, Sublimation, Suppression) to the immature (e.g., Projection, Fantasy)
- At the couple level, introjects from childhood project unrealistic patterns of behavior from one spouse to the other spouse, creating confusion and conflict; introjects from earlier relationships distort all interactions with the spouse
- Aberrant behavior in children results from parental conflict generated by the introjects brought to the current relationship

Assessment and treatment

- Therapy consists of interpreting transference; insight is used to show the connection between current dysfunctional behavior and unconscious patterns (introjects)
- The objective of therapy is to have the individual(s) give up the introjects and construct relationships based on present interactions rather than on residual images from past relationships

Techniques

- Emphasis is on insight
- Verbal working through the unresolved conflicts remaining from early figures of attachment

Role of the therapist

- Therapist attempts to remain a neutral blank slate on which the client can transfer or project the intrapsychic introjects that can then be analyzed and worked through with the therapist
- Therapist attempts to increase the use of mature defense mechanisms among the family members
- Therapist encourages and provides an environment of

safety within the therapy session, thus allowing greater individuation within a family, with freedom to work through residual parts of previous relationships

- The therapist projects a balance of rational behavior and affective expression; this models for the parents proper behavior for handling themselves around their children

Multigenerational Family Therapy

Multigenerational family therapy theorists are similar to object relations theorists in their emphasis on the individual's intrapsychic evolution. Primary differences are the additional emphasis on the multigenerational transmission of pathology and on individuation from the family of origin. The major figure in this model is Murray Bowen (1976; 1978). His work has influenced a generation of well known family therapists; these include Philip Guerin (Guerin, Fay, Burden, & Kautto, 1987), Thomas Fogarty (Fogarty, 1976a,b), Michael Kerr (Kerr & Bowen, 1988), Betty Carter (Carter & McGoldrick, 1988), and Monica McGoldrick (McGoldrick & Gerson, 1985). Two other individuals who can be put in this group are James Framo (1982) and Ivan Boszormenyi-Nagy (1987; Boszormenyi-Nagy & Spark, 1973); however either one could just as easily be put in a general psychoanalytic family therapy category. Within this model, the emphasis on transmission of psychopathology is a result of Bowen, Framo, and Boszormenyi-Nagy's investigations of schizophrenics and their families during the period that their respective theories were being developed.

General assumptions

- Two tenets underlie this model: fusion and individuation
- Fusion or emotional stuck-togetherness reflect lack of individuation from the family of origin; indicated by excessive emotional reactions, and lack of rationality
- There are at least six interrelated concepts that form the basis of this model:

  1. *Nuclear Family Emotional System*—level of emo-

tionality (stuck-togetherness) in the family of origin; high levels produce undifferentiated children

2. *Triangles*—fusion, reflecting anxiety, creates the need between two people to bring in a third to reduce the anxiety; smallest stable unit in family

3. *Family Projection Process*—the process of transmitting levels of undifferentiation to children

4. *Multigenerational Transmission Process*—the process of transmitting decreasing levels of differentiation across multiple generations; the cumulative deficit produces psychopathology (e.g., schizophrenia)

5. *Self-Differentiation*—the process of individuation from the family of origin; maturity is reflected in a balance of rationality and emotion, and immaturity (undifferentiation) is evidence by excessive emotionality, especially during periods of crises

6. *Emotional Cutoff*—attempts to manage unresolved attachments to parental figures (i.e., inappropriate means of lessening fusion); these include moving away, avoiding conversations or topics

- Lack of differentiation in the family of origin leads to an emotional cutoff from parents, which in turn leads to fusion in the new marriage; lack of differentiation produces triangulation of others, projection, or marital conflict
- The goal of therapy is differentiation; the more an individual can differentiate in the family of origin, the better adjusted that person will become; this results in a better spouse and parent

Assessment and treatment

- Genograms are used—multigenerational family maps
- Therapy can last one to two years; sessions may be weekly or monthly depending on the task assignments

Techniques

- Bowen and Framo do family therapy only with couples, and Boszormenyi-Nagy will work with couples or families
- Bowenian therapists will usually work only with one spouse while the other spouse either silently observes or is not present
- The problem is redefined as a multigenerational issue, and spouses are asked to explore unresolved family issues; this may include visits to relatives and family members, writing letters to kin (both living and dead) in an attempt to let go of negative emotion attached to an individual or issue

Role of the therapist

- Therapist serves as the triangulated child, and from that position works toward helping the parents differentiate from the family of origin
- Therapist attempts to stay neutral, and coaches via questions
- Assign tasks to get the individual to develop behaviors to end emotional cutoff

EXPERIENTIAL

Unifying Features

In general, Experiential models are characterized by an emphasis on growth, experiencing and monitoring internal processes, and the development of self within the context of the family. Furthermore, there are several unique therapy characteristics associated with the Experiential models: (1) each person in the family is taught to be responsible for self, and how self underlies all action; (2) emphasis on the expression of emotion during session; (3) spontaneity of affect unencumbered by cognition is encouraged; and (4) therapists are encouraged to share their internal process in response to the session. Although several schools of therapy claim to be Experiential family therapy (e.g., Gestalt Family, Client Centered Family Therapy), their individual deficit assumptions so clearly permeate their techniques that the therapy is basically individual therapy with multiple family members. Within the systems-experiential orientation, models by Virginia Satir and Carl Whitaker clearly represent the interaction of family and self.

Another characteristic of this orientation is that the models tend to be led by charismatic leaders. As a consequence, when the leader dies or becomes less active, the popularity of the model diminishes. Typically, most guru driven models lack clear theoretical guidelines; hence their tendency to decline in popularity with the decline of the leader. However, as evident by their longevity, both the Whitaker and Satir models have detailed writings describing theory and therapy. Interestingly, Whitaker advocates the importance of no theory; he thinks it is an encumbrance to the therapist.

A third, and often ignored, characteristic of this orientation is the written and oral use of verbs, adverbs, and adjectives as nouns. For example, the adjective *becoming* is used to reflect a desired state (a noun); grow and experience are used similarly. In keeping with the spirit of this orientation, I have tried to maintain this linguistic style throughout the Experiential sections of this book.

Whitaker

Carl Whitaker, a traditionally trained psychiatrist, emphasizes therapist spontaneity, creativity, and enjoyment in therapy as a model for family members. This emphasis, often approaching irreverence, along with the lack of emphasis on theory, has made Carl Whitaker a popular figure in the family therapy field. This model clearly has its underpinnings in traditional psychoanalytic thought (Whitaker & Malone, 1953). Others associated with this model are John Warkentin, Richard Felder, David Keith, Thomas Malone, and Augustus Napier.

General assumptions

- Individuals reflect the family; experiencing results from living in a family, and a family teaches the individual how to experience
- By participating in symbolic experiential family therapy, family members become comfortable with their impulses and can integrate them into everyday life
- Dysfunctional families:

    have no integration of the whole

    have not separated in generations

    have little flexibility in power distribution, role structure, and role expectations

    are characterized by their unexpressed emotion, robbing them of flexibility and vitality

    stop growing when they encounter stress

    have difficulty tolerating inconsistency, and life cycle changes (Whitaker & Keith, 1981)

- Health is a continuous process of becoming; crises are opportunities for growth
- Problems arise because of emotional stuckness
- The goal is to increase the sense of belongingness in the family, yet define the unique individualness of oneself; goals are processes
- Growth, not stability, is the goal of therapy; expanded experience leads to growth
- Self-fulfillment depends upon family cohesiveness
- The best way to promote individual and family growth is to liberate affects and impulses
- A climate of emotional deadness leads to symptoms in one or more family members
- Family pathology arises from an impasse in a transition in the family life cycle or in the face of changing circumstances
- Mental health is viewed as a continuous process of growth and change
- Change occurs when family members risk being more

divergent, expressing anger, or greater intimacy (Napier & Whitaker, 1978)
- In general, therapy seeks to increase the separation between generations, to encourage family members to be comfortable with themselves, to expand the symptoms, escalating interpersonal stress, to develop a sense of individual uniqueness that will allow openness to others

Assessment and treatment

- Initial session and contact: Battle for structure—who will be there and what therapy will be about
- Initial session:
  the symptoms are reframed to emphasize the mutual responsibility of all parties
  perspective shifts to show that the scapegoat is no longer the only one associated with the problem
- Battle for initiative: therapist refuses to walk the family through therapy, rather they must decide what to work on; that is, take the initiative
- Anxiety in session is stimulated and prized; it frees the individual from suppressed emotion
- Treatment is generally designed to help individual family members find fulfilling roles for themselves, without over-riding concern for the needs of the family as a whole
- Emphasis is on expanding experience
- Marriage consists of two scapegoats sent out by their families to perpetuate themselves (Whitaker & Keith, 1981).

Techniques

- Psychotherapy of the Absurd: the use of absurdity to change processes of emotional expression, raise anxiety, or encourage general enlightenment
- Personal confrontations/self disclosures
- Symptoms redefined as efforts for growth
- Modeling fantasy as alternatives to real life stress
- Augmenting the despair of an individual family member

- Free associations
- Sharing dreams

Role of the therapist

- Theory stifles creativity and spontaneity in the therapist
- Therapists should spontaneously express their feelings; modeling the things they want to see in the family
- Personal involvement, not technique, enables therapists to do their best
- Therapists should share feelings, fantasies, and personal stories, if that's what they feel like doing—awakens feelings in the client and models
- Techniques are the product of the therapist's personality and the co-therapy relationship
- Co-therapy is necessary to handle emotional tension, and countertransference
- Therapists are caring and confrontive (escalate stress) in a way that encourages growth in the family and its members.
- Emphasis is on therapist enjoying therapy enough to trust his or her judgment to spontaneously say and do the right things in session

Satir

Virginia Satir, a social worker, was initially associated with MRI but later left because of her emphasis on emotion and self-esteem. She quickly found a following in California during the Human Potential Movement of the late 1960s and 1970s. Until her death in 1988, Satir (Satir, 1972; 1983; Satir & Baldwin, 1983) emphasized addressing individual issues in therapy.

General assumptions

- Emphasis on self-esteem, maturation, communication
- By validating individual growth, family members are changed and developmental delays are removed

- Goals are that individuals more fully individuate, which leads to greater intimacy
- The relationship between marital partners is of utmost importance to the family (Satir, 1983)
- Low self-esteem is learned in the family from nonverbal behaviors and remarks parents make in interaction with children
- Assumes that communication patterns reflect the interpersonal functioning ability of an individual (Satir, 1972, 1983); low functioning people tend to overgeneralize

Assessment and treatment

- Individuals with low self-esteem can be conceptualized as belonging in one of four communication patterns: (1) placator—always agreeing; (2) blamer—disagrees, and blames the problem on the speaker; (3) computer—logical without affect expression; and (4) distractor—turns the issue in another direction (Satir, 1983)
- Increased maturity is the goal of therapy (Satir & Baldwin, 1983); also, seeks to develop self-esteem, improve communication skills
- Initial phase of therapy: life history, family of origin, expectations of marriage, life and expectation as a parent
- Second phase of therapy: gets family members to be vulnerable by expressing feelings, wants, desires, and unfulfilled needs. Spontaneity is encouraged. Issues are randomly raised.
- Third phase of therapy: integration of raised issues. Actions are planned for resolving issues.

Techniques

- Used ropes and blindfolds to dramatize the constricting roles family members trap each other into (Satir & Baldwin, 1983)
- Experiential and encounter techniques used in session
- Family Sculpture—family arranges itself using distance and body positions according to various dimensions of the

family like closeness, affect expression, etc. (see Duhl, Kantor, & Duhl, 1973)
- Drama—act out screens from their life
- Reframing (see MRI)
- Family reconstruction—a task using a multigenerational perspective to help teach the individual where faulty learning occurred as roles and expectations have been played out over the years
- Emphasis on "I" statements
- Activities to emphasize awareness of self

Role of the therapist

- The therapist models the skills advocated in therapy— attending, listening, gives empathic responses, and willingly and openly expressing opinions while demonstrating respect for others

SUMMARY

This chapter reviews three orientations to family therapy. Although there are different ways to categorize them (e.g., by techniques, treatment unit), I followed Levant (1984) and divided them by the reference or focus used in therapy, either historical, experiential, or ahistorical process (Levant's Structure/Process). Although each theory sees the family as contributing to aberrant behavior, each uses a different method of altering the family transactions to allow the behavior to be unnecessary. The Historical and Experiential orientations focus much more on the individual, and his or her residual baggage from the family of origin. In contrast, the Ahistorical Process orientation acknowledges, yet is indifferent to the family of origin influences, and instead focuses on how current family interactions maintain the presenting problem. Numerous books and book chapters have been written that compare and contrast the various orientations, and within an orientation, the various models. While each has its own bias, nonetheless, these compare and contrast writings are an excellent source for beginning family therapists to appreciate the theoretical nuances that distinguish the major approaches. A suggested list of these compare and contrast pieces are in Chapter 10: *Recommended Readings.*

5

THE THERAPIST

Often lost among theories, techniques, and tasks is the concept of therapist. As the therapist, you are responsible for eliciting information from strangers and altering their perspective of the problem in a way that creates a change in family interaction patterns. Notice that the emphasis is on you, not on the family. Families are responsible only for implementing changes invoked by you. Their implementation of these requests generally reflects the quality of therapy. Most often, their *resistance* to change reflects inadequate conceptualization of the problem, or inappropriate and unimaginative tasks.

Responsibility for change belongs to the family, the task of instilling that responsibility is the job of the therapist. Within reason, if the family does not change, you should assume that you, as the therapist, did not provide the platform the family needed to make the change. By adopting this mentality prior to therapy, coupled with a good disdain for losing, you elevate therapy to a contest between their dysfunctional pattern and your ingenuity. Dysfunctional family patterns reflect a strategy, albeit typically nonconscious. This strategy must be altered by the therapist. In effect, the good therapist develops a strategy to counter the family strategy. It becomes a noncombative intellectual contest for the therapist.

87

THERAPIST ROLE

The therapist wears at least three hats—cultural healer, artisan, and mental health expert. Each requires a different set of skills, responsibilities, and privileges. As the therapist, you should be cognizant of which role you are providing at any given time in therapy. Depending on the expectations of the client and the therapy process, you should be able to move seamlessly from one role to another.

Cultural Healer

Throughout history each culture has had its designated healers, both physical and spiritual. Until recent times, this privilege fell to the religious men or women within the culture. Little distinction was made between mind and body; any illness, mental or physical, was usually considered a result of displeasing some god or gods. In modern society, physicians now treat physical disorders, and assuming the legitimacy of the duality of mind and body, others, usually psychotherapists, treat the mind. The field of psychiatry, attempting to harness legitimacy within medicine, is increasingly emphasizing biologically based psychiatry, despite the dearth of unequivocal evidence. With this shift away from the healer role, psychiatry has effectively left a vacuum in modern culture.

This vacuum is being filled by psychotherapists of different perspectives and training. Unfortunately, many psychotherapists view therapy as simply a job and do not appreciate their role as a designated healer. As a healer, you have power; you are the modern Shaman. This means that you can do or say most anything in therapy to get behavior change, as long as you stay within accepted ethical parameters. For instance, unlike a normal person in a normal conversation, in therapy you can:

- act "different"

    gaze at someone longer than expected or generally accepted

spontaneously tell stories or metaphors

have unusual speech patterns: slower, faster, answer your own question

- converse about taboo subjects

    sex

    money

    assorted body parts and their functions

- demand compliance and behavior change

    seduce the client into a self-interest behavior change

    gently demand or coax compliance

Remember that, as someone designated as having unique powers or insight, you have leverage with the individual or family. With leverage comes power, and as a result of having this power, you need not restrain your therapy maneuvers for fear that the client will terminate.

A healer also has Presence. Having been given the privilege of knowing the mysteries of human behavior, you must adopt a position of expert. This is not arrogance or one-upsmanship, but the ability to convey an understanding of the problem and the ability to normalize the problem. In session, the therapist evidences this presence through subtle confidence and the ability to structure the session. By determining what occurs in therapy and how it occurs, the therapist brings to the session a presence that is needed to demand pattern change. Without this projected sense of competence, the therapist has a lower likelihood of successful task implementations, which in turn decreases the odds of changing dysfunctional patterns. An excellent perspective on psychotherapist as healer is in E. F. Torrey's (1986) *Witchdoctors and Psychiatrists*.

Artisan

A good therapist is also an artist. Somewhere between the thespian and the used car salesman is the good family therapist. Like the stage performer, the family therapist commands attention through flair, drama, and pacing. And like the used car salesman, the sales pitch is always present, but instead of selling cars, the family therapist is always pitching the interactional perspective, either directly or indirectly.

Like any craftsman working in his or her medium, the therapist strives for a therapy maneuver that embodies simplicity and parsimony. The maneuver should be subtle, but effective. It should not call attention to itself, but merely take the therapy an additional step further toward change, either in pattern or perspective. Any good therapy move is a combination of timing, nonverbals, and a theory-guided verbal statement. Verbal statements are discussed elsewhere (see Chapter VI: *Questions*). Here we are concerned with the art of subtle influence. As a therapist, you are crafting an interaction among individuals for the sole purpose of changing patterns. Simply stating a request is not sufficient for changing long-standing patterns; you must augment your verbals with nonverbals and paralinguistic cues. These cues are delivered as an actress delivers her lines, seeking maximum impact with minimum nuance. This is done by the use of appropriate, yet subtle, flair and drama throughout the session. For example, you use voice modulation, body posture, and eye gaze to emphasize points or to direct interaction.

Another trait of the artist is the ability to determine and modify process as it occurs. Just as the stage comic alters the monologue, depending on what's getting laughs, the good therapist recognizes process (i.e., interaction patterns) as it occurs. By having an idea of what needs to occur, the good therapist has the ability to alter strategies in mid-maneuver, making changes as the situation dictates. There is nothing noble about completing a directive or maneuver if subsequent failure is obvious. A good example of therapeutic flexibility is MRI's discussion of one-upsmanship or one-downsmanship moves by the therapist (see Fisch, Weakland, & Segal, 1982). For example, the therapist usually directs process in therapy, but if that fails, an option is to enlist the help of the family (one-downsmanship) in solving a problem. This flexibility guards against getting stuck in therapy.

Mental Health Expert

One final role is thrust on all therapists—the mental health expert. As defined mental health experts, family therapists are continuously asked to comment on the family and pathology. Family therapists have two responsibilities relative to these questions: first, they should demonstrate knowledge about human behavior, and second, strive to reduce the perpetuation of myths about families and relationships. In the case of the first responsibility, families often ask whether what they are experiencing is normal or abnormal. In most cases, presenting problems seen by the typical family therapist fall well within the bounds of normal behavior. And for the typical family in therapy, if the therapist can normalize the presenting problem, it helps settle fears of abnormality.

People and the media often out seek a therapist for information about the problems associated with being in a family. The individuals usually will ask about the latest trend in pop psychology and family problems (e.g., codependency, inner child). As a responsible professional fulfilling the role of mental health expert, the family therapist should be well read in the scientific literature on the incidence and prevalence of specific family-related disorders. For example, contrary to popular myth, the incidence of child abuse has not risen in recent times (Gelles & Straus, 1987; Straus & Gelles, 1986). Yet the media will often cite supporting quotes from a local mental health expert as evidence to their corroborate their story line. Ironically, most of the necessary information is easily obtainable from any undergraduate family studies or child development textbook (e.g., Eshleman, 1988). Since families assume that therapists are experts, therapists should obligate themselves to maintain a current working knowledge of problems affecting the family.

BASIC THERAPY SKILLS

Normal Social Interaction (with a Twist)

Contrary to what seems to be popular belief among psychotherapists, most families would rather sit and talk to an ordinary person than to someone trained in the mechanics of psychotherapy. It is not difficult to understand why—an average person responds with spontaneity, a well rehearsed psychotherapist responds on cue. An average person smiles, laughs, and disagrees, while a well rehearsed psychotherapist responds on cue. This comparison continues ad infinitum; the format never changes. Despite a long-standing and seemingly respected tradition in psychotherapy, reacting to people in a rote (e.g., tell me more) manner does not enhance therapy outcome (see, e.g., Crane, Griffin, & Hill, 1986). In fact, normal social interaction skills probably better serve a therapist than do several re-readings of Truax and Carkhuff (1967).

A good family therapist can be characterized by his or her ability to direct therapy process, while simultaneously appearing to be holding a normal conversation with the family. Defined here, a normal conversation refers to the bidirectional exchange of ideas and pleasantries. The trick for the therapist is to maintain the air of normal conversation, yet direct process through the use and timing of nonverbals, paralinguistic cues, and verbal statements (see, e.g., Birdwhistell, 1952).

Manipulating nonverbals and paralinguistic cues, the therapist, as artisan, has to direct the therapy while appearing to be in a normal mid-afternoon conversation with a good friend. There are several discrete things that the therapist can manipulate to facilitate the process of therapy. They are:

- Voice

    Forceful yet moderate tone, not wimpy; avoid sounding like a therapist
    Modulate voice
- Intermittent Eye Contact

Break to force attention, and return as you complete the
sentence

Look when listening; force their attention toward you

- Spontaneity

React as you would in a normal conversation, not as a
therapist

Respond with interest; therapy is an intellectual
challenge—enjoy it

- Drama and Flair

Eyes—communicate with them; smile with them
(Ekman & Friesen, 1984)

Hands—wave them to make or exaggerate a point

Voice—exaggerate as needed to make a point

- Humor

Use to fluctuate or alternate mood as needed

Laugh to provide an air of normal interaction to an abnormal situation

Use self-deprecating humor to move to a one-downsmanship position

Use satire, gently

- Body Position

Sit in a position comfortable to you

Lean forward to emphasize a point

Lean back out to let the family or couple talk

Be active; move to complement your voice and gestures

- Linguistic Structure

Pause to emphasize points, to force attention to the next
word, or when delivering a task or an idea

Make short statements

Avoid talking too much; say only what is necessary; most
therapy time is filler joined by therapeutic moves

Think first, form the sentence, then deliver the statement

Learn indirect hypnosis techniques (Zeig, 1980;
O'Hanlon, 1987)

SOCIAL NEGOTIATION

As noted throughout this text, a core component of family therapy is altering the perspective of the family from an individual deficit model to an interpersonal model. This alteration begins with the first contact and proceeds through termination. The success of altering the perspective is dependent on your skills as a negotiator. You first determine what they believe, and then you decide what you need them to believe in order to change the presenting problem.

By using verbal and nonverbal skills, your task, in effect, is to allow the family to view the presenting problem in such a way that it is interactional and fixable, and that its presence does not indicate pathology. The easiest way to do this is to view their perspective as a malleable entity. As such, the job then is to use your skills to mold the entity (Minuchin, 1979). First, you join the family (see Minuchin & Fishman, 1981), build a coalition, and then modify. Modification occurs when you state a position that you need, and they accept; or, if they disagree, you back up, agree that their perspective is possible, and then offer an alternate possibility that is slightly different than the first you offered. This alternating process is continued until the family or individual is viewing the situation in a manner consistent with your needs to change the dysfunctional patterns. Your willingness to listen to their perspective and seemingly back up invokes the norm of reciprocity, and they will eventually entertain your ideas. This concept, albeit in abbreviated form, is illustrated in Figure 4.

As your style of negotiating with a family evolves, you develop a skill for knowing when to agree, when to disagree, when to be antagonistic, and how to use humor, along with all the other skills used in social intercourse. You will become increasing comfortable using manipulated interaction to allow a family to see the presenting problem as something other than an individual with a deficit.

Figure 4: Altering the perspective of the presenting problem.

THERAPIST AS ENGINEER

As you adopt the relationship model, think of yourself as a structural engineer brought in to fix a construction project gone awry. You have been asked to consult on an ongoing project in which the original blueprints have been lost. Your objective is to provide the construction crews with an idea of how to continue building the structure. Initial fixes (tasks) may not eliminate the problems, but they provide you with additional information about earlier construction, current construction techniques, and the quality of construction crews. You determine, for example, the skill level of the crew, whether or not the crew is overworked, if there is a crew leader or leaders, or even if the current problem is a result of previous efforts to fix the problem. You further assume that with your input the crew has most of the necessary skills, tools, and materials to fix the problem. If initial attempts to repair the problem fail, you assume that your directions were unclear or that you missed several vital bits of information about the structure; this will be remedied on the next round of suggestions. This process is continued until the crew has successfully completed the structure.

WHAT TO AVOID

Two things to avoid during a therapy—arguing with the client and robotitis.

Arguing with the Client

Given that the objective in family therapy is to change behavior patterns and perspective, it is imperative that you do not argue with the client. This is not in reference to negotiating a perspective, but if the client makes a point of stating a position, either overtly or metaphorically, listen. Often, the family or individual will describe a belief or myth, sometimes veiled as family behavior, that is incompatible with what you want to do with the family. Although bothersome, it still does not warrant opposition.

A simple axiom—*if you argue, you lose.* If the position is incompatible with the objectives of therapy, bide your time and slightly alter the position in small increments. If you argue, especially overtly, you lose power, and power determines leverage. Without leverage you will not get compliance.

Robotitis (robo-titis)

This is a common affliction among therapists, and is easy to catch. Its characterized by flat affect, lack of facial spontaneity during therapy, and ritualized speech (e.g., *Tell me more about that* or *How do you feel about that?*). Definitive diagnosis occurs when the client checks for the therapist's pulse.

Fortunately, Robotitis usually responds to autosuggestions about enjoying therapy and to removal of all thoughts that family therapy necessarily implies the need for miracles.

SUMMARY

To be a therapist means you have been designated a cultural healer and mental health expert, with the right to be an artist. This means you have rights, privileges, and responsibilities that extend beyond normal social convention. Most importantly, you have been given freedom to do and say things in session that will alter the perspective of individuals and families. Accepting this responsibility entitles you to use your techniques to improve the quality of life for these individuals by providing a way to solve their problems.

Verbal and nonverbal skills enable you to change the meaning of the presenting problem. How you say something and what you do while talking are as important as what you say.

Avoid Robotitis.

6

QUESTIONS

In many respects, techniques represent the penthouses of therapy. They sit atop the theoretician's view of how the world should look. These intricate and mysteriously designed bits of wizardry embody the theories they represent. Yet their high visibility makes them vulnerable to abuse through imitation. While imitation connotes flattery, it seldom produces good therapy. Although important, techniques simply reflect theory. For the beginning therapist, it is much more important to think, and then speak, consistent with a theoretical position than it is to regurgitate tricks from a text. The clearest way to convey your thoughts is through speech. And the easiest way to illustrate your perspective in therapy is through questions. Questions form the basis of good therapy. They generate information, alter perspectives, and allow change. Moreover, by their structure, questions can provoke and gently antagonize the family without direct confrontation. This allows faster access to the family's belief system.

THE FUNCTION OF QUESTIONS

Questions have three functions: they reflect therapist perspective, they request change in an interactional manner, and they alter client perspective. Any given question can emphasize a specific function or, as in most cases, encompass all three.

Reflect Therapist Perspective

Questions provide the therapist an opportunity to imply an interactional perspective as a rationale for the presenting problem. Question phrasing is an extension of the therapist's thinking. If the thinking is interactional, the questions will address interaction. For example, below are two questions that imply that the therapist assumes that an interactional pattern maintains the presenting problem and that the individual can control the presenting problem.

> *To the father:* How does Sally lessen her tantrums when you spend your afternoons with her?
> *To Sally:* How do you know when to have a tantrum?

Such questions add doubt to the family's assumption about Sally's inability to control the symptom, while offering the family a new perspective about the maintenance of the tantrums.

Request Action in an Interactional Manner

As a natural consequence of asking questions from an interactional framework, change should also be requested from the same perspective. If the therapist has slowly coaxed the family toward an interpersonal perspective, then transitioning from requesting information to requesting change is a natural progression. In question form, the request for change usually occurs outside of a specific task. Questions use indirect requests that involve at least two family members, or an individual and his or her context. For example:

- What are some of the ways he would act differently if you changed your response to him?
- If you left your room clean, how much longer do you think you mother would let you play outside?

Alter Client Perspective

As the therapist redefines the problem as interactionally based, the client is allowed to perceive the problem differently. Since the interactionally based problem assumes no individual deficit, each family member is assigned a role in the dysfunctional pattern, and each is expected to fulfill that role given the dynamics of the system. By asking questions in a manner that conveys this perspective, and with enough therapist pervasion and negotiation, the family comes to adopt the thinking as their own.

TYPES OF QUESTIONS

Information Seeking

Information questions have two goals, to gather information and to shift the perspective away from the individual toward context and interaction. For example:

- What else is going on at home that may be tied to Johnny's behavior?
- How does Johnny's behavior get worse when you fail to be consistent on the rules?
- On days when you're upset about your marriage (or your job), how does Johnny's behavior change?

Initial attempts to shift the perspective will usually prompt the individual or family to remind you that tho IP (identified patient) has the problem. Do not disagree, simply present yourself as naive and then ask another question, only slightly less interactional. Most individuals or families quickly adopt an interactional perspective when they are not forced to, or if there is only a minimum-to-moderate investment in having the presenting problem reside in the IP. In fact, most families will readily acknowledge some contribution to the presenting problem, especially parents who feel guilty.

Ask the question in a manner that describes a current malleable pattern, which, if agreed on, you can fix. Conversely, do not discuss or entertain the idea of the presenting problem being a result of a historical event, or even a current non-malleable pattern. For example, consider the mother with very inconsistent parenting who also drinks too much, which she attributes to her marriage that ended six years ago. Assuming that the drinking is a convenient way to avoid parenting and the previous marriage is a convenient reason to drink, ask: *How is Johnny's behavior affected by your drinking?*, not, *How is Johnny's behavior influenced by the problems in your first marriage?* The first question deals with the interaction between the mother's current behavior and Johnny's presenting problem, whereas the second addresses a vague set of issues in the mother's past that she uses to avoid responsible parenting. Although it could be argued that the mother's drinking stems from some unresolved grief from the first marriage, from the family therapy perspective this notion is seldom invoked. Rather, the idea of functionality is pushed to the forefront as a reason for displaying incompetence. In this scenario, the first marriage is merely a handy excuse to drink. Now, first marriage or not, the drinking may be difficult to stop (see, e.g., Steinglass, Bennett, Wolin, & Reiss, 1987), but that's a different issue.

To illustrate that this is not a hypothetical extreme, consider the words of an actual client who says, "How can you expect me to fix dinner for my kids, or see that they get a bath each night, when I still need to work though the trauma of having been sexually abused in my first marriage?" This statement was made by an unemployed single mother of four children, who was basically overwhelmed by her life situation, and whose children were suffering as a result. Fortunately for the children, the debilitating effects of the first marriage on the mother lessened dramatically following a visit from the local Child Protection Agency.

Rhetorical

Rhetorical questions illustrate a pattern and, in so doing, solidify a shift in perspective. These rhetorical questions are used as if you are simply verbalizing your thoughts, maybe to someone specific, or maybe not (see section below on who gets the question). Done in this manner, the rhetorical question is not stating a fact or asking for change, but merely suggesting the possibility of how things might be viewed. For example:

> Assume that Mom, Dad, and Johnny are in the session and you direct this question to Mom: "How do you suppose Johnny would talk to you differently if his dad spent more time with him?"; or you could ask the mother, "When your husband doesn't yell, how does Johnny's behavior change, for better or for worse?" Remember that you are not looking for an answer, only suggesting what might be. Then, immediately turn to Dad and ask, "If I were to let her answer, what might she say?"

This sequence of questions puts Johnny's behavior, metaphorically speaking, squarely in the middle of Mom and Dad. Addressing the last question to Dad allows him to defend himself, thus legitimizing the possible scenario. (Note: the father's response is irrelevant, the therapeutic work was done with the question.)

Hyperbole

Exaggerating a point makes the acceptance of a less extreme position more palatable; in some situations, it allows the therapist to indirectly address the dysfunctional pattern without invoking a disagreement from the family or individual. Always use humor. For example:

> *To the parents:* "Well you now have two kids. Neither listen to what either of you say. Why at this point in your parenting career are you contemplating joint parenting?" This instructs the parents to join forces, unlike the past.

> *For the single parent who doesn't want the responsibility of being a parent:* "You're just starting to learn how to par-

ent effectively, and your kid has a three-year head start on being a kid. "Why not forget the hassle, do what everyone else is doing, and just hire a nanny?" This nudge allows the parent an opportunity to express how he or she wants to teach the child, and that he or she could do a better job than a stranger. To this you say, "Yes, that's right."

Behavior Change

One primary function of any question is the request for change. These questions are interwoven into the conversation, and typically are not used as a behavioral assignment. As questions prompt a different way of looking at the problem, the structure of the questions moves from general to specific. They evolve from an "It is possible" perspective, to a "What if you . . . (specific interaction)." If the specification is sufficiently clear, change should occur *spontaneously* between sessions. In fact, if questions prompt behavioral changes that coincide with a perspective shift, then very few formal tasks are needed to change relevant patterns. This means that assigned out-of-session tasks can be requests for small discrete changes in the dysfunctional pattern, insuring a high probability of success. This, in turn, provides concrete evidence that therapy is progressing.

Asking for behavior change can be either direct or indirect. Direct is easier, but more likely to bring forth reasons the behavior cannot be done.

Direct request for change

When directly asking for behavior change, structure the question in such a way that it *implies* compliance. In this way, any response almost seems like a binding contract, without your telling what to do. For example:

To Mom: "The fastest way for Sally to get your attention is by picking on her sister. How will you *not respond* the next time Sally *tries* to provoke you?"

Indirect request for change

Indirect requests for change rely on ambiguity. This type of question is intended to provoke some confusion, or maybe to get the client to think about the presenting problem in a slightly different way. For example:

> *To the mother, with both parents present:* "I don't think that your husband can stop reacting to Johnny's taunts, what about you?" Is the therapist asking the mother her opinion about the father's ability to change his reaction to Johnny or about her own ability to stop reacting to Johnny? The ambiguity prompts the mother to consider the possibility that either she or her husband, or both of them, need to stop reacting to Johnny's taunts, without being directly told to do so. Similarly, the father must consider his behavior relative to his wife's opinion of his ability to handle Johnny's taunts.

HOW TO ASK QUESTIONS

Basic Components

Before any question is asked, mental rehearsal is absolutely necessary. The question should be well conceived, short, and to the point. *Impact is inversely related to length.* Even if the desired influence is indirect, the question should be direct (see the example above).

Each question has both a proximal and a distal function. You form the question to be appropriate in the ongoing conversation; yet, the question and the response establish the perspective shift that reflects therapy objectives and, to a large degree, the outcome. As each question is being formed, two criteria should guide the construction:

1. What do I need?

    If the question is to gather information, ask yourself:

What information is necessary to form an educated guess about the dysfunctional interactional patterns? Decide beforehand what you need to know (i.e., what is useful; e.g., Structural—boundaries & heirarchies to implement therapy). This is dictated by theory.

If the question is not strictly to gather information (e.g., Rhetorical), ask yourself: What answer do I need that will either solidify a point that I am making or take the individual or family to the next stage of changing perspective? In most cases, other than strictly information gathering, you should already know the answer, and you form the question in a way that provides the needed answer. *The question is simply a linguistic maneuver to get said what you need in order to continue therapy.* If you think of therapy as a sequence of predetermined moves having a cumulative affect, then responses to questions provide the substance needed to progress from one step to the next.

To illustrate, consider the situation where you need the father to increase parenting. First, he needs to think that his parenting affects his son's behavior, and then, more specifically, that his lack of involvement is detrimental to the boy's development. This implies that the father first needs to recognize that fathers, in general, influence the behavior of their offspring. Then, more specifically, that his lack of parenting has adversely influenced his son. To accomplish this progression, you first need several general questions about fathers, parenting, and kids. For example, "How do kids learn how to behave?" and then, "How do kids, especially boys, learn appropriate behavior from their fathers?" Irrespective of the father's response, you take some part of it, and reinforce or alter as necessary to support your point, and then move to the next question. In the next series of questions, you focus on how the father's lack of involvement has hampered the development of the son's social competence. For example, "Let's assume that Johnny's problem may be, at least in part, due to your lack of direct influence. How do you think he would be acting differently today had you consistently spent more time with him?"

This primes the father for the next question: "Given your insight into the role of fathers and your ability to influence Johnny, how will you change the way you spend time with your son?" Notice that the father was not told what to do, which might promote some animosity, but, was instead nudged in a direction toward more parenting. Then he was asked what he was willing to do to show change. Almost any verbal response by the dad implies an obligation on his part.

2. What perspective shift is necessary?

At the minimum, assume that from the moment that you meet the client, you will be slowly shifting the perspective toward interpersonal and away from individual pathology. This shift becomes more intense and overt as you determine what part of the system you want to draw attention to and what pattern you want to change. As therapy progresses, the structure of each question should foster and extend the interaction perspective. This structure should be consistent with, or slightly ahead of, the individual's or family's current grasp of the pattern. In effect, the therapist pulls the family toward the desired interpersonal perspective via the structure of the question. As such, sentence structure must be well developed before the question is verbalized.

Assume, for example, that the mother acknowledges that her interaction with her daughter greatly influences the daughter's disposition. Being aware that the father refused to attend therapy, and assuming that his behavior in the present context is typical of other situations (i.e., lack of involvement), you then extend the mother's perspective to include Dad's influence and their (as a couple) joint influence. You might ask, "While your behavior with your daughter certainly affects how she acts, how does her dad's behavior influence her behavior—no—more importantly, how does her disposition get *worse* when you and your husband sometimes disagree?" The latter section of this question is very general, almost astrology-like, and will invoke little disagreement by the mother. It has the effect of moving and broadening the mother's perspective, and it establishes a rationale for father's needed attendance in therapy.

Question Format: Reference Domains

In therapy, questions and answers occur in three reference domains: affect, behavior, and cognition. Each makes reference to the presenting problem and dysfunctional pattern from a different perspective. In traditional psychotherapy, affect responses hold an exalted position, as if to imply that referencing affect is more therapeutic than referencing either of the other two. This empirically groundless assumption, probably derived from the *Physicalism* movement of the 1850s (see Chapter 2: *Intrapersonal vs Interpersonal Models*), limits the therapist to a single domain. In truth, affect is merely one of three domains, each having unique properties that can be exploited, depending on the therapist's needs.

Question Format: Open

Begin with a broad general format (e.g., *How, Tell me*) and narrow to a specific connection that you want addressed (e.g., *He does X and you do Y*). This type of format forms the bulk of the questions asked, and is appropriate for information, hyperbole, rhetorical, and behavior change questions. Responses by the individual or family are usually broad enough to provide the therapist with information about the suspected dysfunctional patterns. Most often, these questions begin with, or focus on the words, *How* or *What*.

Consider, for example, when the therapist is initially attempting to alter the perspective of the family from the preconceived notion of pathology to an interactional perspective. Thus, the question needs to address both the presenting problem and the perspective shift. As the questions move from a general outline of possibility to a specific sequence, the shift in perspective should be evident. The attempted shift in each question should move slowly enough so that you simply appear to be gathering information, not necessarily implying that a causal relationship exists. A series of questions might look like this:

- When does Johnny hit?
- Whom does Johnny hit?
- How does Johnny know when to hit?
- How does Johnny's hitting change when you are around?
- How does your yelling escalate Johnny's hitting?

Of course, in a real therapy situation, the questions would have been preceded with a discussion of the hitting and some hint that the yelling may precede the hitting.

After a series of questions linking yelling and hitting, the therapist could ask, "What needs to change in this family for you to be willing to yell less?" This distributes the dysfunction across the family, implies that the individual can control the yelling, and simultaneously begins to establish therapy goals.

Question Format: Closed

The role of closed questions is limited to a few very specific uses in therapy. Most often, closed questions are used to force a client to agree or disagree with a position that the therapist is trying to establish. Their construction usually limits the response to a yes or no, and they are seldom used to gather information. Most importantly, do not ask the question unless you are almost absolutely sure of the answer. They are useful for solidifying a perspective shift, and usually begin with *Why, Do you,* or *Don't you.* Often, rhetorical questions are asked in closed form. For example, to solidify the position that joint parenting is necessary you might ask the couple, "Don't you think that if the two of you could jointly decide what is, and is not, acceptable behavior it would be such a relief to Johnny that his behavior would almost immediately improve?"

Question Format: Who Gets the Question

The therapist has to make a strategic choice about whom to ask the question, and when. It will have a differential effect depending on who is specifically addressed and who is *allowed* to hear it. The options are:

- Address the whole family
- Direct to one member, heard by the whole family
- Direct to one member, but specific to another member
- Remove everyone but the one member you want to talk to

If you elect to remove family members from the session, assume information leakage will occur. Utilize this by asking the question as if it will later be conveyed (in a slightly altered form) to another family member. This is especially useful when you are dealing with an adolescent whom the parents are likely to ask what was said when they were not in the room. You can predict the questioning and, either overtly or covertly, rehearse an answer with the child. If you need to form a coalition with the child, this covert activity increases leverage with the child that may be useful as therapy progresses.

SAGE QUESTIONS

Some questions appear particularly insightful. Clients respond immediately with a smile of approval, or with flat affect, followed by acknowledgment of the legitimacy of the comment. These are Sage questions. Despite the name, mere mortals can produce these questions with regularity. Steps to developing a Sage question are:

1. Observe the family or individual in detail, noting especially the behavior and method of thinking unique to the individual
2. Have a very good grasp of the presenting problem and its associated patterns of interaction
3. Take careful note of how the client is responding to questions, look for consistencies in thinking, and from where (metaphorically) the answer comes (e.g., a belief system)
4. Think ahead of the client, anticipate answers to questions or responses to statements
5. Once a pattern is clearly evident, jump the next two logical questions and ask the question that was third in line to be asked

Consider, for example, the case where the older adolescent cannot hold a job, and must therefore live at home. When you talk to the parents, it becomes obvious that their marriage is distressed, especially for the wife. The son provides Dad with company and companionship, at a cost of social maturity for the son. Rather than slowly working toward the marriage, the therapist decided to move into the relationship quickly after it became evident that the wife would support any therapeutic forays into the relationship. In the second session with the parents, and after about 20 minutes of discussing the son's behavior, I asked Mom, "What will be the cost to your marriage if your son is able to hold a job?" After a brief pause, the response was, "We wouldn't have one!" At that point, family therapy became marital therapy.

If the question was on target, you appear insightful. These Sage questions are extremely important for establishing interpersonal leverage that may be subsequently needed to get a person to stop, or start, a behavior. In other words, by appearing insightful, you appear competent, thus earning the right to make demands on the individual or family.

If the question is not on target, you get the "Where did that come from?" look from the client. Do your best Peter Falk (Columbo) imitation (e.g., Gee whiz, I'm not sure what I was thinking), then go back two steps and continue. There is nothing inherently wrong with making this kind of mistake, except that making too many will cost you therapeutic leverage.

One very clear way to avoid making mistakes when asking these questions is not to be led by theory bias, but rather to let the individual's or family's mode of thinking dictate your questions. *Assume only that the problem is interactional, nothing more.* Do not assume, for example, that the father is peripherally involved and the mother is overly involved with the child, or that someone with this presenting problem must have been sexually abused. Such biases are therapy blinders. Let the client's responses and perspective of the problem determine what you ask.

MEANINGLESS QUESTIONS

Meaningless questions can be classified into two types, redundant and empty. Neither type provides information, makes a point, or alters client perspective. In the short term, they stop the flow of therapy; over time, their lack of substance sabotages therapeutic efforts to implement change. As a therapist, you should be specific about the information *you want*, the answers *you need*, and how the *family should perceive* the distressing behavior.

Redundant Questions

Redundant questions are those asked by the therapist that seek information already provided by the individual or family. By asking for information that has already been given, either directly or indirectly, the therapist appears insensitive to the dynamics in the family. If this happens often enough, the family loses confidence in the therapist's ability, not to mention in his or her short-term memory. Conversely, the therapist appears most insightful by merely restating as true what has already been indirectly mentioned or alluded to by the family members.

This is an example of a redundant question:

The father says, "I hate it when she refuses to answer me!!" To which the therapist replies, "What does she do that bothers you?"

A better question would be:

"How can she tell (pause) from your behavior (pause) that her refusal to answer gets to you; what do you do to let her know?" This generates interactional information for the therapist and allows the father to see how her behavior is tied to his predictable response.

Empty Questions

Empty questions generate information that you cannot, or will not subsequently use in therapy. This category includes cliché questions or questions that elicit information from the wrong reference domain.

Cliché (brain-dead) questions:

These questions include the generic questions used by Hollywood scriptwriters, pop psychologists, and brain-dead therapists. Most prominent among these questions are the ubiquitous, *How do you feel about that?* and *Tell me more about that*. Although the latter is not a question, it attempts, albeit in a non-specific way, to elicit information from the individual.

In the case of *How do you feel about that?*, this question is usually asked immediately after the individual has clearly expressed (either directly or indirectly) how he or she feels about the issue, which, ironically, probably prompted the question initially. This question usually creates two problems: first, the therapist is asking for an affective response, which is fine, except that the response is not tied to an interaction or context, and contextualization is necessary to subsequently alter client perspective. Second, the therapist should decide prior to asking the question whether he or she needs an affective response, a behavioral response, or a cognitive response. Each requested reference domain provides the therapist with a different type of information that will be used later, and each domain response alters the client's perspective in a different manner. For example, supposing the therapist wants an affective response, then, "How do feel when you think Johnny deliberately ignores you?" prompts the mother to identify feelings that accompany a specific behavioral sequence. For a behavioral response, the therapist could ask, "When you get angry at Johnny for pretending to ignore you, what do you do next?" A cognitive perspective question might sound like, "What are you thinking when Johnny pretends to ignore you?"

The other most common vacuous request, *Tell me more about that*, is actually worse than the first. It seeks anything and answers nothing. You should be very, very specific about what you want and how you want it. As a therapist, you are seeking the specific information necessary to compose a workable perspective for the client—one that is interactionally based and provides a solution to the presenting problem. For example, the therapist might ask, "Tell me how you will let Johnny know that his yelling, which was successful previously, will no longer get you to give in." This forces the mother to acknowledge (1) that Johnny's yelling was being reinforced, (2) that she will change, and (3) that she will let Johnny know about the change.

SUMMARY

Questions are second only to the conceptualization shift as the most important component of learning to be a family therapist. Depending on why and how a question is asked, the therapist can generate information while simultaneously shifting the individual or family to an interactional perspective. Questions are used throughout therapy to simultaneously request change and probe the family system. Questions permit more humor and subtle sarcasm than direct statements. Avoid empty, redundant questions.

Unfortunately, the general format of these questions can be learned without understanding what the questions are doing. Although the questioning method and underlying thinking described in this chapter are slightly different from the circular questions used by the Milan group, they nonetheless are very similar. An excellent overview of the Milan questioning technique and conceptualization for the use of questions can be found in Fleuridas, Nelson, and Rosenthal (1986) and Tomm (1985).

7

THERAPY
IMPLEMENTATION

DOING GENERAL FAMILY THERAPY

This chapter is written as a general and practical introduction to family therapy. It combines the various Ahistorical Process models. Theoretical purists would, and should, be disgruntled by this combination. However, since this is a practical introduction, and not an academic exercise, I think this combination works best for therapists first learning family therapy. It is easy to grasp conceptually and does not require a new vocabulary, only a conceptual shift, and in general gets results (Gurman, Kniskern, & Pinsof, 1986). This combination is typical of how family therapists actually integrate models because of their functionality and apparent results. Moreover, this text is intended as an introduction to ideas more than to model specific techniques. Greater specificity can and should be gained by reading, in detail, the original and contemporary writings for each family therapy orientation.

Finally, the purpose of this book is to illustrate how to think about a presenting problem, and then, based on a few simple assumptions, how to verbally and nonverbally act in-session to increase the odds of changing the presenting problem. There is no emphasis on correctly labeling behavior according to some model or orientation, only on altering the behavior pattern and its concomitant mental perspective.

THERAPIST RESPONSIBILITIES AND THERAPY OBJECTIVES

The objective is to change the presenting problem by changing the pattern producing the undesired behavior. The optimal method of changing behavior is to allow the pattern to change—don't attempt to force it. As therapy begins and patterns become evident, the therapist is continuously revising an internal monologue consisting of *"what if"* I do this, or *"what if"* I do that. These mental gymnastics reflect strategies that are constantly being revised in order to better conceptualize the relevant patterns and anticipate ways to avoid failure. To avoid failure consider:

- Who will oppose?
- What part of the intervention will they oppose?
- How can I circumvent the expected opposition?
    schedule the expected opposition
    describe to the family, in great detail, the expected process of opposition

As a therapist with an interactional perspective, you must take responsibility for inducing change, both in behavior and perspective, that leads to alterations in patterns of interaction. If therapy is not progressing as expected, then the following dimensions of therapy are continuously addressed:

- What am I not seeing?
- What did I do wrong?
- How am I not phrasing the questions correctly?
- How was the task incorrect or inadequate?
- Given partial results, what next?

PRESENTING PROBLEM PARAMETERS

In family therapy there at least three features about the presenting problem that need to be examined: (1) timing, (2) function, and (3) person. Each provides a piece of the puzzle.

Timing

Always ask yourself *why now*? What has occurred recently or, if not recently, how long ago? What was going on in the family when this started? Why wasn't the behavior present yesterday or last week? What is occurring now that makes the behavior necessary for the individual? Were there changes in the family or larger environment when the problems started? Were there job changes, separations, fights, and so on prior to the onset? These questions can be asked directly or indirectly. Indirectly would be something like, "Give me a picture of the family, and how it has changed over the past year," or "Describe the family's everyday routine for the past six months."

Function

Ask yourself as each individual describes the presenting problem, "What is the *result* of the behavior?" Similarly, as they interact in the session and describe the presenting problem, ask yourself at the individual, parental, and family level, "What gets accomplished and what does not get accomplished?" Accomplished here means any personal or interpersonal activity that should occur in a functional family. These include, for example, developmental changes, relationships, work, or individual activities.

Person

As a result of the behavior, who directly reacts to the behavior, and as a result of the reaction, what happens? Reaction means attention, action, or general response. When the behavior occurs, what is the next response? Consider Johnny, the biter. When John bites Jane (the sister), who reacts, how do they react, does John get more or less attention (than before the bite), do bites occur most often when Mom and Dad are fighting, or have they increased since Mom and Dad separated? This is the internal scenario that you need to develop in order to grasp the sequence of interaction surrounding the presenting problem.

Although this example illustrates a short-term (hours or minutes) behavioral sequence, the thinking is equally applicable to sequences that cycle through over a period of days. This extended perspective can be illustrated by the child who regularly threatens suicide. For example, the child threatens suicide, Mom calls the crisis unit, everyone converges to the scene, and Mom and child have a very different relationship for some extended, yet temporary, period.

BELIEF STRUCTURE

Changing the dysfunctional patterns that produce the presenting problem is the object of therapy. All techniques are driven by this objective. You seek to simultaneously change the presenting problem, either directly or indirectly, and the cognitive perspective that necessitates the dysfunctional interactions within the environment. In family therapy, this cognitive perspective is a belief structure maintained by the family, with slight variations held among the individual family members (Bagarozzi & Anderson, 1989; Reiss, 1981).

This family-level cognitive perspective acts as a filter, determining the meaning of events, which in turn dictates reactions to the events. For example, depending on the family's history and culture, events are interpreted according to beliefs held by the family. The beliefs, or myths, may be functional or dysfunctional. They may be functional in their ability to keep the family intact, and yet to the world outside the family be dysfunctional in the type of behavior that the beliefs produce. Similarly, treating an individual within the interactional perspective assumes that he or she has a cognitive perspective that influences the perception of environmental input, and determines that individual's behavioral reaction. At the couple level, Weiss (1980) refers to this as sentiment override.

In effect, because of these beliefs, family therapy seeks to alter the belief as well as the behavior. However, depending on the family therapy orientation used, the therapist may seek to change the belief either directly or through a change in the presenting problem. In other words, you can change the behavior and assume that it will allow the belief to be less valid and subsequently unnecessary; or you can attempt to change both simultaneously. Either way, the presenting problem must change, and its underlying belief structure must be altered enough to allow the dysfunctional behavior to be unnecessary. Questions and suggestions offered in this book illustrate how behavior and perspective are changed at the same time.

DIMENSIONS OF FAMILY THERAPY

Phases of therapy typically refer to periods of the therapeutic process characterized by distinct shifts in therapist behaviors, goals, and maneuvers. Although in several family therapy orientations this position is still maintained (e.g., behavioral; Alexander, 1988), the notion of discrete shifts in the family therapy process is a misnomer. More specifically, in this book, it is assumed that the therapeutic process begins at first contact, and from that moment on, the distinction between assessment and prescribed change is blurred as these interdependent dimensions continuously address the presenting problem. Instead of thinking of therapy changing over time (e.g., phases), it is better to think of therapy as containing three interdependent dimensions occurring simultaneously over the period of treatment. They are assessment, instilling doubt, and pattern change. A description of each is given below:

Dimension I: Assessment

This includes determining relevant behavioral patterns and belief systems in the family. Assessment occurs throughout treatment, and the therapist's concept of the problem is continuously updated from information via questions and responses to tasks. Assessment is in two areas: interaction patterns and belief structures.

Behavioral interaction patterns

- Who does what and when? (see Chapter VII: Questions)
- Who responds to whom, when and how?

Family belief structure

- How does the family think, in the sense of a singular unit; what themes are present?
- How is the family hierarchy related to these beliefs?
- Where are the family alignments & coalitions (Minuchin & Fishman, 1981)?
- What is the language of the family, and how does it reflect their beliefs?
- Beliefs and myths about causality

    bad genes ("His uncle was a troublemaker")
    biochemical imbalance ("Something is wrong with him")
    supernatural—God, devil
    friends ("If he had better friends, he would not do those things")
    differential parenting ("His mother is not strict enough")

- Beliefs and myths about the cure

    reverse the causal agents (e.g., find new friends)
    medication
    somebody else changing

Dimension II: Instilling Doubt

Simultaneous to assessment, the therapist begins the process of subtly casting doubt on the validity of the family's current belief system about the presenting problem. Seldom will the family acknowledge that marital or family interaction patterns produce the presenting problem, or even that the problem lies outside of the child. Typically, you have to slowly address the interactional and contextual dynamics surrounding the presenting problem.

This occurs in several ways:

- questions (see Chapter VII: Questions)
- reframes (see Chapter IV: *Family Therapy Orientations: MRI*).
- directives for in-session interaction (e.g., enactment; see Minuchin & Fishman, 1981)

This process begins immediately in the first session, and continues unabated throughout the treatment period. Initially, it serves to alter the presenting perspective to allow change in dysfunctional patterns, and later serves to concretize the new ideas about how and why behavior occurs. During initial sessions, several additional components must be introduced into the therapy process to insure that the client is willing to make the effort to change (Fisch, Weakland, & Segal, 1982). These components are:

- Parent's expressed willingness to change

  Your objective is to get a verbal contractual agreement from the parent(s) that they will work to change whatever is necessary in order to remove the presenting problem.

  State to the parent(s) : I will work with you if you will do what I ask.

- Parent(s) must assume some responsibility for the change

  You must get an agreement from the parent or parents

that they will assume greater responsibility for changing the presenting problem. This may need to be done indirectly, at least initially, through questions and reframes. This removes the therapist from the role of miracle worker, and puts the focus back into the family system.

- Make explicit the effort necessary

  State that there are no quick fixes

  There must be parental consistency for all rules, across all family members

  All members in the home will be held accountable for their behavior; this includes lovers, friends, and family

- Make explicit the consequences of not changing

  Problem may improve, but probably not (Kazdin, 1987; Patterson, et al., 1992)

  Things that could happen (depending on the problem): expelled from school, substance abuse, jail, pregnancy

These four components should be conveyed early in treatment, especially after you have a grasp of the dysfunctional patterns that you want changed. Moreover, the first two components, parental commitment to change and acceptance of some responsibility, must be obtained early in treatment, and without qualification. Without this commitment, therapy will fail.

Dimension III: Pattern Change

Family therapy exists to remove problems. Problems are embedded in patterns, and patterns are determined by context. Family therapy, then, exists to alter context. From this viewpoint, the job of the therapist is to alter the context driving the behavior, while simultaneously using the presenting problem as a handle to manipulate the context.

This dimension of therapy is characterized by implicit or explicit requests for change in the patterns that are associated

with the presenting problem. Using the removal of the presenting problem as the goal, you must make decisions about what
needs to be changed and how to shift the belief structure to
allow the desired behavior to occur. Although the presenting
problem is held as the defining reason for being in therapy,
short-term goals for smaller, less volatile behavior are often
used to coax the individual or family toward more desirable
behavioral patterns along with an altered family belief structure. This implies that as assessment is occurring and doubt is
being cast upon the existing beliefs, you offer opportunities for
behavior change.

These opportunities occur both in and out of session.
In-session opportunities occur when verbal statements by the
therapist prompt a slightly different perspective (e.g., using
questions), or when requested tasks force the family to interact
differently. Out-of-session opportunities occur when behavior
tasks are implemented. These requested tasks may include parents negotiating curfew times or having the parents decide on
consequences for misbehavior. The requested task forces new
interactions around the presenting problem. When any task is or
is not completed, the response to the task by each individual
provides additional information used by the assessment dimension (see Tasks below).

TASKS

In-Session vs Out-of-Session

Tasks, or requests for specific behaviors, can occur either in
or out of session. In-session tasks consist of directing the interaction among family members. This can consist of interaction
between family subunits, or among members as a whole. Out-
of-sessions tasks usually are thought of as homework assignments. Irrespective of family therapy orientation, most
therapists use both types.

In-session

In-session tasks often are associated with the Structural school of family therapy (Minuchin & Fishman, 1981). However, the experiential exercises used by Experiential family therapists can also be thought of as tasks (Satir & Baldwin, 1983). As used by the Structuralists, and other ahistorical proponents, the in-session task has three functions: (1) it allows the therapist to see relevant interaction; (2) it allows the therapist to alter relevant interaction, and (3) it allows the family to experience new patterns of interaction. Observing interaction in a session is extremely beneficial in determining what is occurring in the family and how it needs to be changed. Assuming that the in-session behavior is isomorphic to the out-of-session behavior, the therapist is confident that what is seen reflects what happens in the home.

These tasks can be as simple as asking the husband and wife to talk about relevant issues, or as complex as having a family meeting on some topic. Each task, irrespective of complexity, generates relevant interaction needed for continuous assessment. As discussed elsewhere, theory dictates what is relevant. For example, as outlined in the *Theory & Techniques* chapter the therapist always attends to:

- What is *gained* by the presenting problem(s)?
- Who gains by the presenting problem(s)?
- What is its function relative to family patterns, or structure?
- How does it maintain the existing pattern?
- What are the consequences of the presenting problem(s)?
- How is the presenting problem defined?

    By actual behavior
    By family committee
    By family myth

- Who reinforces or confirms the definition?

    Other families with similar problems
    TV talk shows; media; self-help books
    The use of medications

Other mental health workers

- What makes the behavior a problem?

    Is it the behavior?
    Is it the timing?
    Is it the consequences?

- For whom is it a problem?
- What patterns need to be altered?
- What is the temporal level of intervention?

    moment to moment
        - immediate responses
            extended period
        - days, weeks

- What structural changes need to be implomented?

    Combining subunits
    - Joining mother and father
    - Joining siblings
    - Joining child with peers
    Dividing units into subunits
    - Separate parent and child
    - Form therapist coalition with each
    Points of therapeutic leverage in the family
    - Does the IP view the behavior as a problem?
    - Do all parties view the behavior as a problem?
    - Who gains by not viewing the behavior as a problem?
    - Who is most invested in change?
    - Who is least invested in change?
    - Who can be the best ally?

Another value of the in-session task is that it provides the therapist with the opportunity for the family interaction pattern to fail at its assigned task (Minuchin & Fishman, 1981). For the therapist, there are therapeutic benefits in observing the family fail at the assigned task. Specifically, observing a failed task:

- Provides information about the pattern structure
- Provides immediate opportunity for therapist to comment on the process
- Provides an opportunity to challenge the belief system

Some families benefit more than other families from in-session compared to out-of-session tasks. Because in-session tasks generate new interactions among the family during the session, they are especially useful with families characterized as chaotic, that is, where most family members have infrequent, or volatile contact with other family members. This also includes families where the lifestyle increases the likelihood that the family will come for only one or two sessions. Finally, in-session tasks may be necessary for families that fail, for whatever reason, to complete out-of-session tasks. These families should be given in-session tasks to determine what interactional components contribute to out-of-session failures.

Out-of-session

Tasks that request specific changes in behavioral interactions outside of therapy are the hallmark of the strategic and behavioral therapies (see Chapter IV: *Family Therapy* Orientations). A given task has the singular function of altering, however slightly, familial interactions that are consistent with removing the presenting problem. Out-of-session tasks require interactions that need time, opportunity, or situations that are outside of the therapy session. These might include hardship tasks (Haley, 1984) or positive interaction opportunities (e.g., movies), or they might need several days or weeks to complete (e.g., parent monitoring of child behavior). Moreover, if the task fails, the out-of-session task allows the therapist to determine the sequencing of behaviors associated with failure.

As with in-session tasks, failure to complete out-of-session tasks is seen as a source of information within the assessment dimension of therapy. In turn, the failure information is used to devise and reassign another, slightly modified task. This next task accounts for the previous failure by modifying important ingredients in the interaction; if successful, this takes the pattern closer to the objective. If the task again fails, even with the modifications, then the therapist has more information about what is interfering with change. As an aside, if your tasks fail regularly, stop assigning tasks until you can determine what is contributing to the failure—what it is about how you made the request, what the task requires, or what you are not noticing about the family that would have predicted the failure. Or else, when the family reports why they failed, tell them that you had predicted the failure. In response to their, "Why did you think it would fail," offer them a perspective of the problem such that had they completed the task, the presenting problem would be unnecessary, or at least, it would have forced the presenting problem to occur in a slightly different form. This not only makes you appear smart (i.e., cover-your-posterior move), but indirectly ties the pattern of noncompliance to their desire to remove the presenting problem. In effect, you put pressure on them to comply with subsequent requests for change.

Finally, do not assign tasks without a reason. Often we feel compelled to have the individual or family do something, anything that might change the presenting problem. Such compulsion effectively puts the cart before the horse. Change comes not from the task, but from the quality of the therapy relationship— that composite of intangible bits of behavior and nuances during interaction that permit a perspective shift in the client. Tasks simply allow the perspective shift to manifest itself behaviorally. In effect, the task demonstrates that behaviors can be changed in accordance with the prescripts of therapy. In some cases, no tasks need to be given; in others, the therapist gives a task at each session. Whether or not to assign a task depends on what the therapist determines the family needs. Since the needs of families vary, so should task assignment. In any case, assign a task only if the family needs one, not because books (such as this) say so.

Task Assignment: Written vs Oral

Out-of-session tasks can be either written or oral. Written tasks are usually done by behaviorally oriented family therapists. Nonbehaviorally oriented family therapists seldom write out the task except when the paper itself or the list of expected behaviors is symbolic. In effect, then, the list of expectations has symbolic meaning beyond the assignment, and the therapist is more concerned that the client has the task literally in hand than in the implementation of the requested changes.

Written contracts are especially good for single parents who have abdicated their parenting responsibility in exchange for the child's friendship. A written list of needed behavior changes, along with consequences for noncompliance, forces the mother to be responsible for parenting the child (Patterson, 1971). If a well developed contract has been negotiated and the parent will not accept the responsibility for parenting, this abdication becomes evident very quickly.

An often overlooked aspect of behavioral family therapy (BFT) is that in the hands of a competent family therapist, contract negotiation is family therapy. Specifically, good contract negotiation requires detailed information about the presenting problem. You need to know when it occurs, how it occurs, what precedes it, what follows, who is involved, who is not involved, and when it does not occur. This is the same information needed in practically all the ahistorical approaches. In effect, negotiating a contract forces the family to identify patterns of interaction. This detailing of reciprocal actions forces acknowledgment of complicity in the problem and, in turn, works toward effectively altering the family's perspective. To successfully implement a family contract, all members must change their behavior, which is the general objective of family therapy. In fact, it could be argued that *negotiating* a behavioral contract has a monitoring effect and is probably as important to behavior change as is successfully *implementing* the contract. On the other hand, BFT overtly details the dysfunctional interaction pattern, while other models may or may not be so explicit. Whether or not to be explicit depends on the individual style of the therapist and on what is most likely to facilitate change.

While written tasks rely on specificity, oral tasks tend to be more general. Underlying this generality is the idea that the individual, couple, or family has the inherent capacity to implement the changes within their environment without the aid of a written contract. For example, in an attempt to involve Dad, the father is to check the child's room nightly for completed chores. The therapist simply says, "Dad, you will be responsible for checking Johnny's room by 9 o'clock each night." Such a broad statement assumes that Dad has the capacity to objectively check the room, which may or may not be the case; irrespective, Dad is given the chance to demonstrate competence. If he does, a portion of the larger behavioral pattern has been changed; if he does not, the subsequent task is altered slightly to provide another opportunity to demonstrate competence.

Whether written or oral, tasks require behavior change at the pattern level. Written tasks utilize greater specificity of action and reaction, whereas oral tasks depend more on the assumed internal capacity of the individual members to respond appropriately, given the opportunity.

Compliance vs Noncompliance

For any task, either written or oral, the therapist needs compliance. Compliance allows the family or individual the opportunity to change behaviors. This behavior change runs concurrent with, or precedes, the desired perspective change. Compliance also elevates the status of the therapist; each successful effort to change behavior reinforces the utility of therapy for the family. It follows, then, that the therapist should only request a task that has a high likelihood of being successful. It is a mistake to request a task that is likely to fail. Stated differently, don't ask until you are sure you will get success. While this sounds simple, it actually is. Success is dependent on the observational skill of the therapist to grasp the location and behavioral mobility of each individual within the system. Most individuals or family members will telegraph their exact location within the pattern you are trying to change, and each will tell you how much they will move within that pattern. Always ask for change that is at the very edge of the limit expressed by the client. Move the family in small bits toward the desired interaction pattern. If the steps toward change are too large, you insure failure, and if they are too small, you waste the client's time and money.

A final word about tasks—they are useless without a reason. Family therapy reflects a house built on techniques and tasks. Unfortunately, books, videotapes, and workshops make it appear as if these are the things that change behavior. They do not. They only provide opportunity for new behavior to occur in accordance with the ongoing therapy. In other words, tasks and techniques serve as vehicles for change; the impetus comes from the therapy. This position can be easily verified by watching the novice Structural family therapist have the family members move their chairs (because Minuchin does) without rhyme or reason. While such ill-timed moves effectively confuse the family (and supervisor), it does little to alter family functioning.

FIRST CONTACT

A typical first contact in family therapy occurs with a telephone conversation. In addition to the usual information about location and fees, the family therapist also includes additional information about:

- Who should be present

  Try to get everyone relevant to the presenting problem. This includes all adults in the household and all siblings. Although you may eventually do therapy with everyone, you might also only bring in subunits. However, in the initial session, you want everyone. Each individual brings unique information about the family beliefs and the presenting problem. If all else fails, get whom you can.

- Framing the treatment expectations

  Address questions about format and expectations in terms of family contribution to the process of behavior change. Assert that all members of the family must be available to attend if needed by the therapist. Be frank about the assumption that family problems are related to the entire family, not solely to an individual. It is better to lose a client initially because of ideological differences than to have them come in and be disappointed in the treatment.

- Avoid implying causality

    As you discuss expectations, avoid implying that the family caused the presenting problem; suggest only that the family is necessary to fix the problem. Also avoid giving the caller any hypothetical ammunition that can be taken back into family and used to blame someone, as in, "The therapist said it was probably your fault that Johnny is acting this way." In essence, be vague and state that you will need to see everyone before any comments can be made.

WHO IS PRESENT IN SESSION

Recall that in the interpersonal model you are doing therapy with the pattern, not the person. As such, you need only those family members (or relevant members of the system) who provide the leverage to alter the interactions that need changing. Stated differently, you need in therapy those subsystems that allow you the ability to change the relationship. And who you need may change from moment to moment within a session and across sessions. Do not be afraid to shuffle people in and out of the therapy room if doing so generates leverage, or if the act of excluding someone mimics metaphorically the desired changes (see Minuchin & Fishman, 1981).

Conversely, sometimes the needed individuals will not or cannot attend therapy. Although not optimal, since therapy is with the relationship, intervene as if your actions will ripple through the system. Actually, you should always assume that any action taken in therapy will percolate among the relevant parties. Therefore, structure all tasks as if the person in therapy is both the client and the messenger. This dual role for the client is usually not made explicit unless the act of making the role overt is itself the therapeutic maneuver. You might, for example, tell the acting-out adolescent to stop breaking curfew (a desired behavior) long enough to determine if the parents "are really serious" about lifting other restrictions. Assume that the adolescent will hint to the parents their obligation to reciprocate his actions.

FIRST SESSION

During the first session, your objective is to join with the family (Minuchin & Fishman, 1981), assess the problem, and begin altering the family's perspective.

- Joining (Minuchin & Fishman, 1981)

    Reciprocate pace of speech and word usage
    Use humor
    Avoid the look and sound of a prototypical psychother-
        apist
    Move slowly as you gather information

- Assume that family interaction defines the family system:

    Attend to process (see Chapter III: *Theory & Techniques*)
    Attend to nonverbals
    Attend to affect: its occurrence, nonoccurrence, timing
    Listen to content for cues of language usage, beliefs,
        myths, and perspectives; *what* is said is less impor-
        tant than *how* it is said.

- Assessment of the Problem (see Chapter III: *Theory & Technique*)

    Perspective from each family member
    Gather history: how long, when, where
    Determine the role/function of the behavior
    In-session tasks if necessary

Include and exclude family members as needed; do not let members stifle or interrupt others

- Determine limitations and pace of client movement

  Do not press too hard or too fast
  Build allies among family members least invested in change

- Do not require a behavior change task unless you are absolutely sure that it will be successful, and you already know how the new behavior will integrate into the therapy plan

SUBSEQUENT SESSIONS

Subsequent sessions build on the initial session—shifting perspective and changing behavior. Each therapeutic maneuver either sets up or implements small changes that are consistent with eliminating the presenting problem. These small behaviors are, in fact, short-term goals; in turn, success in these short-term goals inexorably leads to changes in the presenting problem. Changes, as defined here, refer not only to interaction patterns, but also to shifts in the client belief structure. Remember, the shift in perspective refers to a method of *allowing* the individual or family to see behavior in a slightly different way. Allowing is the key word. Clients are not told that their thinking is wrong (see, e.g., RET—Ellis, 1975), or that their reality filtering process is faulty (see, e.g., Cognitive Therapy—Beck, 1976), but rather, emphasis is on the *possibility* that faulty interaction patterns produce the dysfunctional behavior. Specifically, efforts are directed toward changing the behavior via interactional tasks while concomitantly asking questions about, or indirectly making reference to, the beliefs that underlie those interactions.

In general, there are no prescripts about what to do in any given session other than always to guide the client to change. Each therapeutic maneuver should be goal-directed; each should attempt to alter pattern, perspective, or both in relation to short-term goals. And in turn, each short-term goal must be directly related to the long-term goal of removing the presenting problem. For example, a short-term goal might be getting the mother and father to view the son in a slightly different way. You might want to have them see him not as a "sick" kid, but as a son reacting to a chaotic home life. A series of small moves such as this eventually allow the parents to take more responsibility for the environment that shapes the child's behavior.

ADVANCED STRATEGIES

Although this book is intended as a basic text, there are several strategies that need to be mentioned that are typically employed by therapists who have seen families for several years. First, as you move people (give new roles, new beliefs, etc.) within the family in order to allow changes in behavior, position them within the system so that when you ask (metaphorically speaking) that the presenting problem no longer be necessary, each family member will act as if the presenting problem were nothing more than a mere nuisance anyway. This can be done if you follow a simple rule: *For every behavior or belief that you alter or take away, give the individual a new, less dysfunctional one.* Your objective is to change interactions such that no one clings to, or needs, old behavior patterns when new ones are introduced. Experience, gained from observing and interacting with a large number of families, will eventually yield insight into what roles individual or family members need as changes are requested.

A second advanced strategy is sequential questioning. Sequential questioning occurs when you ask questions, knowing in advance the answers, that move the individual or family in a specific direction of change. Sequential questioning can take two forms: the "Yes" set version and the "Chess" version. In the "Yes" set version, you establish a "yes" set by asking two or three questions that have "Yes" as the answer, with each question logically connected to the other. After the "Yes" set is established, ask a final question that forces a small, but distinct conceptual shift. For example, suppose an acting-out boy is brought in by the custodial mother joined by the noncustodial father. A history indicates the boy's behavior is much worse at school and home during the first few days following weekends with Dad. Mom and Dad continually fight when together. The following is a "Yes" set that shifts the problem away from Johnny, and toward the interactions that instigate Johnny's behavior.

Therapist to Father: Has Johnny's behavior reached an almost intolerable level?
Father: Yes
Therapist: Will it continue to get worse if something doesn't change soon?
Father: Nods yes.
Therapist: Do you want it to stop?
Father: Of course!
Therapist (delivered slowly): Do you want it to stop bad enough to change the way you talk to him about your ex-wife (pause) and his mother?

This ties Johnny's behavior to the parental conflict, and tells Dad how he can change things.

The "Chess" set of sequential questioning gets its name from the process of using a series of inter-related and predetermined questions separated by functionally inert responses by the client. In other words, the therapist knows what direction he or she wants to take the session, and moves the client in the desired direction by asking a series of questions that are graded approximations to the desired goal (analogous to chess moves). Answers are usually irrelevant unless they move the conversation in a direction opposite to where the therapist is going, but good questions insure that this does not happen. Using the above scenario with Johnny, Mom and Dad, the therapist wants Dad to appreciate his contributions to Johnny's behavior problem. A series of questions might take this form:

Therapist: Dad, I know that you and Johnny's mother have talked about this, but can you tell me what Johnny does on these Mondays and Tuesday that gets him into so much trouble?

Dad: (describes what Johnny does—therapist basically ignores what is said, but listens for words or phases that permit an introduction to the next question)

Therapist: So, from what you've been told, Johnny doesn't show his mother much (pause) respect? (the therapist adds "you've been told" since it happens only at Mom's house, and the therapist ignores Dad's specific comments and substitutes the word "respect").

Dad: (therapist attends to Dad's comments and nods appropriately)   .

Therapist to Mom: How does Johnny show you disrespect?

Mom: (therapist attends to Mom's comments and nods appropriately).

Therapist to Dad: (slowly asked) Is Johnny's expressed disrespect for his mother more or less than your expressed disrespect for *his* mother?

This series of questions should take 10–12 minutes to complete. Filler is added by clarification, and requests for additional information as they answer each question. Regardless of the answers, in the "Chess" set, the anticipated moves by the therapist are made according to what the therapist needs to happen in therapy to meet short-term goals. In some respects, answers are by-products that provide the platform for the next question, e.g., they provide words, phases, and stylistic components that allow the therapist to introduce the next question as if it were a natural extension of the given answer. The therapist can either ignore the answers, in effect, and proceed as planned, simply adding bits and pieces into the next question to make it appear as if the question naturally follows the answer, or construct the question in such a way that the question can be answered only in a way that is consistent with the direction the therapist is moving and thus naturally leads to the next question in the sequence.

A third advanced strategy is to use stories and metaphors as agents of change. While a detailed account of how to use meta-phors in therapy is beyond this book, a brief foray into their utility is warranted. For thousands of years, metaphors have been used to teach, to induce a perspective shift, and to change behavior. The prowess of a metaphor is in its ability to circum-vent the normal scrutiny typically applied to incoming infor-mation (Kopp, 1971). When it is properly delivered, people react to a metaphor by suspending normal critical evaluation, and absorb the message without concern for detail. In fact, substan-tial shifts in perspective can be introduced without invoking a defense of the current perspective (see, e.g., Zeig, 1980).

The key to using metaphors, stories, or anecdotes as an advanced strategy for behavior change is confidence. The will-ingness to use metaphor depends on how comfortable you feel using nontraditional methods to alter (or manipulate) the ther-apeutic process. Confidence is not something that comes with experience. With experience, you merely get older, but with confidence you get better.

Advanced strategies have one common characteristic: each provides a mechanism for rapidly, yet indirectly, moving a client toward the desired goal. And each strategy follows a basic rule: have all the roles and all the family members in place before you make any big moves.

DEVELOPMENTAL STAGE OF THE FAMILY

All therapeutic maneuvers must attend to the developmental stage of the family. This includes considering not only the ages of the children, but also the ages of the parents. Parents of a young child face a very different set of problems than do the par-ents of a preadolescent, an adolescent, or a young adult living at home. At each stage of development, individuals within the family have tasks and expectations that influence their behavior. Collectively, these expectations influence the expression of the presenting problem. Each stage of the parenting process is made more complex by the impact of the marital relationship. Single parents handle parenting situations differently than married parents, and happily married couples handle parenting problems differently than unhappily married couples.

In family therapy, the therapist should be cognizant of how the family arrangement and stage influence the patterns that maintain the presenting problem, and how each can affect treatment success or failure. No single recommendation can be made for each possible combination of family stage by family composition, marital status, parenting skill, and so on. Instead, it is much better to examine each family as a unique composite having its own history and belief system. When this belief system, as expressed through behavioral patterns, is observed, the proper therapeutic intervention becomes evident for each family, irrespective of developmental stage.

TERMINATION

Since the object of ahistorical family therapy is to remove the presenting problem, therapy should be terminated when that objective has been met. Some family therapy orientations, especially those with psychodynamic origins (e.g., multigenerational), have broader, yet more vague, criteria for termination. By maintaining a very specific objective, like removing the presenting problem, all parties involved work toward a common goal, and everyone is aware of the changes that have been made or need to be made in order for therapy to be successful. Therapy should be as brief as possible. Some individual or family problems require only 2–3 sessions, others 15–20 sessions. Length of treatment is usually inversely related to the degree of cooperation from relevant family members and the length of time the presenting problem has been present. Unless otherwise evident, it is assumed that in order for the presenting problem to be unnecessary, the belief system must have also changed.

Moreover, implicit in the ahistorical mentality is the assumption that when an individual or family is allowed to interact without the presenting problem, the system will restablize in a less dysfunctional way. This implies that, other than follow-ups at three or six months post-treatment, the job of the therapist is to remove himself or herself from the lives of the family members as rapidly as possible after the presenting problem abates.

Clients, not therapists, should be given credit for any changes that occur during treatment. If therapy is done properly, the family leaves therapy with the presenting problem under control and, more importantly, a sense that they have the inherent ability to handle future situations and problems. This perceived ability to handle future events is not something that is stated explicitly by the therapist, but is rather a sense of ability instilled by the therapy process. The most important way to insure that the family obtains this sense of competence is to successfully shift the perspective of the presenting problem away from the individual deficit and toward a controllable interaction. Given that the new perspective emphasizes context, this shift, in effect, allows individuals to perceive problems as overt and manageable, rather than covert and beyond control.

Finally, the attitude of the family at termination should be that they knew all along what was needed, yet somehow got stuck and were unable to get the job done. At termination, if the family have forgotten how they viewed the world previous to treatment, and now seem confident in their ability to handle future situations, and if they do not assume that it was merely the therapist's ability that changed things, then therapy is successful.

FAILURES

Despite the impression given by most books, videotapes, and workshops, failures do occur, and with regularity. One way to reduce the number of failures is to screen clients selectively, including only those who are happily married, have adequate income, are highly cooperative, and present with a problem that has only recently started. If you, like most other therapists, do not have this luxury, then assume that some families cannot, or will not, be helped by family therapy. Moreover, barring a genetic or organic basis, there is no evidence that if a family does not respond to family therapy another form of treatment will be more effective.

The goal of the therapist is to minimize failures by learning from mistakes, and to set realistic goals for families based on their ability to change. For example, failure is certain if you expect a low-income single mother to immediately institute radical parenting and lifestyle changes in three sessions just because her 12-year-old is acting out in school, and the child's behavior is not viewed as a problem by the mother. Therapy must accommodate the situation and context, and within that accommodation, it should attempt small but significant changes.

While it is easy to blame the clients, their lifestyles, or their unwillingness to change as the cause of failure, most therapy failures, I think, occur because of the quality of therapy.

More specifically, therapy tends to fail when:

- The therapist straddles the conceptual fence—that is, simultaneously holds to the individual deficit model and attempts family therapy
- The therapist demands change in behavior patterns without using the language of interaction (provides no perspective shift); results from straddling the conceptual fence
- The therapist does a poor job of initially joining with the family
- The therapist is too passive; does not demand change
- The therapist is determined to do a task or technique despite contrary information given by the family; numerous task failures insure therapy failure
- The therapist does not project a sense of presence in the session; no sense of artistry
- The therapist has no sense of direction in therapy, leads to unconnected questions; both therapist and family sense the floundering
- The therapist acts like a therapist, not like a real person
- The therapist fails to use humor

It is obvious from the above list that I firmly place responsibility for the opportunity for change in the hands of the therapist. Aside from extreme cases with long-standing problems, which have a low chance of success with any method of therapy (Kazdin, 1987), an active-interactional based family therapist characterized by a sense of presence, a good use of humor, and knowledge of where to take therapy typically will have a moderate to high rate of success irrespective of presenting problem.

DEPARTING COMMENTS

Often it is said that families (or individuals) "need" x or y to get better. X in this case may be the resolution of grief or unresolved conflicts, improvement of self-esteem, the ability to express their feelings, or any number of often prescribed remedies. Such remedies are intended to repair some hypothetical psychological construct. In other words, individuals are told they "need" to fix something that exists in theory only, a difficult task indeed.

These remedies can be implemented by a plethora of techniques (i.e., talking through or about the event, or even reexperiencing the event). Given the paucity and inadequate quality of empirical support for such remedies and their associated techniques, to state that families "need" these treatments is both preposterous and presumptuous. Remember that families or family members "need" only what the therapist was taught in graduate school; hence, what is "needed" depends in large part on where and when the therapist went to school.

In reality, we do not know what families "need." What we do know is that some modalities of treatment have been shown to be effective in treating specific disorders (e.g., BFT [Patterson] ->Antisocial boys). Yet it has been argued that this does not mean that these treatments are more effective, or that other, non-evaluated treatments are not as effective, but rather that the evaluated ones are effective—nothing more.

Until we empirically determine what families "need," it is best to distinguish between what we were taught they "need" and what has to occur in therapy for the presenting problem to go away. *When in doubt, which should be often, always pre-scribe what is necessary for problem amelioration.* And if your prescription for problem removal is *also* what they "need," give credit to the theory. If they are not the same, simply assume that, contrary to the evidence, the theory you were taught is nonetheless correct, and that the client is somehow abnormal.

8

MISCELLANEOUS TOPICS
Supervision, Ethics, and Organizations

SUPERVISION

The practice of marriage and family therapy, and the supervision and training of marital and family therapist are interdependent. In the early 1960s live supervision, the one-way mirror, and the consultation team as co-therapist became synonymous with family therapy and family therapy training. Liddle (1991a) provides a comprehensive overview of family therapy supervision. He details the evolution of family therapy supervision, its critical issues, and current theoretical positions on supervision and training held across the major approaches. Early classical works include Montalvo (1973), Haley (1976), and Cleghorn and Levin (1973). These works established the foundation for modern family therapy supervision associated with university and postgraduate training institutes found throughout the United States.

There are several features of supervision that deserve mention because of their uniqueness to family therapy. First, there is the assumption that, if possible, supervision should be live. Depending on the theoretical orientation of the supervisor and equipment available, live supervision might include in-room visits by the supervisor, being called out-of-session to consult with the supervisor, instructions being telephoned into the session, a bug in the ear, or a collective statement from the consulting team. Irrespective of the theoretical orientation, live supervision via a one-way mirror is considered the fundamental form of supervision in MFT programs in America. Live supervision allows the supervisor to observe the family and the trainee, and to make use of the situation to implement change in the family. Often the line between supervision and treatment is blurred because the directed intervention is intended to teach the trainee and simultaneously alter family interaction. This lack of distinction is exemplified by Milan's uses of the consultation team to generate hypotheses and write prescriptions.

Second, few if any contemporary family therapy training programs require personal therapy of the trainee prior to his or her becoming a therapist. The mentality of the psychotherapist requiring psychotherapy is a residual from the psychoanalytic model that requires an individual to undergo psychoanalysis for the purpose of removing any individual deficit prior to doing therapy. Such a perspective is antithetical to the systemic notion that any behavioral problem exhibited by a therapist probably reflects a contextual problem, not an individual problem.

Third, few training facilities use co-therapy as a means of learning family therapy. Accumulative evidence has shown that co-therapy is no more effective than a single therapist (Gurman, Kniskern, & Pinsof, 1986) and is less cost effective. For the strategically oriented therapist, a co-therapist may actually get in the way of therapy.

Finally, within family therapy, most supervisors assume that the supervision process is isomorphic to the therapy model. Isomorphism implies concordance between the training methods and the methods used in therapy (Liddle, 1988). This implies, for example, that the supervisor is aware of and utilizes the structural relationship between supervisor and student by intervening in a way that increases skills consistent with the model being taught (Haley, 1988; Liddle, 1988; Storm & Heath, 1985). Stated differently, the supervisor questions the therapist about behaviors in the therapy session in the same way that the therapist should be questioning the client(s) in session. In effect, being isomorphic means that the supervision behind the glass reflects how therapy should be occurring in front of the glass.

As expected, each model of family therapy adopts different positions on supervision, training, and isomorphism; good readings on this subject are in Liddle (1991a), and Liddle, Breunlin, and Schwartz (1988).

ETHICAL CONSIDERATIONS

For me, there are two types of ethical issues. the first reflects ethical behavior consistent with the dictates of the professional organization, and the second involves the propagation of constructed illness for financial gain (sometimes referred to as mortgage therapy). In family therapy, the first issue is simple. First you read the AAMFT Code of Ethical Principles for Marriage and Family Therapists (1991), paying particular attention to the following areas:

- Competency—know your limitations; do not assume competence beyond your training. You must, however, first assume that you have limitations; unfortunately, some therapists do not (e.g., a psychiatrist in Phoenix was self-promoted as an expert on hate crimes, the mental processes of freeway shooters, and violent behavior resulting from hot weather).
- Observe Confidentiality
- Duty to warn—you have the duty to warn (the intended victim) if there is a clear and present danger that the client may harm someone else; or if the person intends to commit suicide, you have a duty to attempt to stop that individual
- Dual relationships—simply put, *do not* borrow money

from, do not take stock tips from, and most important, *do not* have sex with your clients

The second type of ethical issue is less clearly defined, hence more evident among unscrupulous therapists. The range of constructed illnesses has reached *epidemic* proportions with the increased availability of insurance and the mass marketing tactics of private psychiatric hospitals. Attracted by simple greed, these entities have enticed many therapists to tell individuals and families that they suffer from a disease. Any particular disease will do (e.g., sexual addiction, codependency, 2nd-order post-traumatic stress disorder) as long as the insurance is current, the psychiatric facility has beds available (note: availability of beds and insurance are interdependent), and it seems to be politically correct (PC). Pittman (1992) provides a humorous account of these PC diseases and their implications for treatment.

Without question, however, the perpetuation of such constructed illnesses is unethical. The process of disease construction not only insures additional client fees, but almost always impedes behavior change, and ultimately allows the client the option of not having to be responsible for his or her current behavior. Recall the mother discussed earlier in the text who said her abuse in a former marriage prohibited her from caring for her children. This abdication of parental responsibility was granted to her by a therapist.

While this book was in preparation, a new, previously undiscovered aliment was sweeping the Phoenix metropolitan area (local media suggest that it is a national problem as well), and can best described as the "I can't be responsible because I had forgotten that I had been sexually abused as a child" syndrome. Affecting both men and women, the syndrome is characterized by complete amnesia to any childhood abuse. It always manifests itself while undergoing therapy with one of a few select local therapists who have either extremely brilliant diagnostic skills or no ethics. Unfortunately, it seems that most of these sufferers were recovering codependents, or some other previously constructed malady. In almost every case that I have seen, therapists making the diagnosis either had an ongoing group for similarly afflicted individuals, or else they referred clients to local psychiatric hospitals where the therapist stood to gain financially (e.g., floor privileges).

Unfortunately, this type of unethical behavior is pervasive. Diseases and diagnostic categories change with economic and political whim, and the individuals and families with the problems typically remain unchanged, except being poorer and stigmatized with a label. In many ways, this institutionalized unethical behavior is more damaging than violations of the tenets listed initially.

PROFESSIONAL ORGANIZATIONS

Although there are numerous professional organizations that attract family therapists, only two are exclusively dedicated to the practice of marriage and family therapy; they are the American Association for Marriage and Family Therapy (AAMFT) and the American Family Therapy Academy (AFTA) (see Broderick & Schrader, 1991). Although a number of people belong to both organizations, they serve very different purposes and different audiences. AAMFT is the largest (approximately 20,000 members at this writing), and is oriented toward the general practice of marital and family therapy. AAMFT is also responsible for accrediting marriage and family therapy training programs in the United States.

Also during the last decade, AAMFT has had a very strong lobby interest in national legislation efforts that affect the family and the practice of marriage and family therapy. Toward this later objective, AAMFT has been extremely influential in mobilizing state AAMFT organizations and their legislators to create licensing and certifications bills that designate the practice of marriage and family therapy as a distinct mental health discipline. Thus far they have been very successful in a very short period of time; currently 29 states legislate the practice of marriage and family therapy. Finally, AAMFT has two levels of membership—associate and clinical, and a separate designation for an Approved Supervisor.

AFTA is a much smaller organization. It is composed of mostly doctoral level senior clinicians, theoreticians, and researchers. Its goal is to further the field of marriage and family therapy by addressing contemporary issues about the family, marriage, and behavior change in a forum of yearly meetings and in the AFTA Newsletter.

9

RECOMMENDED READINGS

BOOKS

Throughout this book I have included a variety of references on each topic. Below are a few references by area that are specifically recommended for someone learning family therapy. These provide a foundation for doing family therapy. References were selected based on their attention to theoretical clarity and implementation of therapy fundamentals; provocative works should be saved for later reading.

Basic Introduction

Foley, V.D. (1974). *An introduction to family therapy*. New York: Grune & Stratton.

Goldenberg, I., & Goldenberg, H. (1991). *Family therapy: An overview* (3rd ed.). Pacific Grove, CA: Brooks/Cole.

Gurman, A. S., & Kniskern, D. P. (1981) *Handbook of family therapy*, Vol. I. New York: Brunner/Mazel. Selected chapters:

Framo, J. L. *The integration of marital therapy with sessions with family of origin* (pp. 133–158)

Kerr, M. E. *Family systems theory and therapy* (pp. 226–264)

Bodin, A. M. *The interactional view: Family therapy approaches of the mental research institute* (pp. 267–309)

Aponte, H. J., & VanDeusen, J. M. *Structural family therapy* (pp. 310–360)

Gordon, S. B., & Davidson, N. *Behavioral parent training* (pp. 517–555)

Gurman, A. S., & Kniskern, D. P. (1991) *Handbook of family therapy,* Vol. II. New York: Brunner/Mazel. Selected chapters:

Broderick, C. B., & Schrader, S. S. *The history of professional marriage and family therapy* (pp. 3–40)

Falloon, I. R. *Behavioral family therapy* (pp. 65–95)

Segal, L. *Brief therapy* (pp. 171–199)

Colapinto, J. *Structural family therapy* (pp. 417–443)

Hoffman, L. (1981). *The foundations of family therapy.* New York: Basic Books.

Levant, R. (1984). *Family therapy: A comparative overview.* Englewood Cliffs, NJ: Prentice-Hall.

THEORY—BASIC

Steinglass, P. (1987). A systems view of family interaction and psychopathology. In T. Jacob (Ed.), *Family interaction and psychopathology: Theories, methods, and findings* (pp. 25–65). New York: Plenum.

THEORY—ADVANCED

Bateson, G. (1972). *Steps to an ecology of mind.* New York: Ballantine.

Bateson, G. (1979). *Mind and nature.* New York: E.P. Dutton.

Gray, W., Duhl, F.J., & Rizzo, N.D. (1969). *General systems theory and psychiatry.* Boston: Little, Brown.

Keeney, B.P. (1983). *The aesthetics of change.* New York: Guilford Press.

von Bertalanffy, L. (1968). *General system theory.* New York: George Braziller.

Weiner, N. (1961). *Cybernetics, or control and communication in the animal and the machine.* Cambridge, MA: MIT Press.

AUTHORS/TECHNIQUES

Always try to read the original writings first, then move on to collected works, and finally, overviews or summaries. Below are a few recommended readings per model that compliment the suggested introductory readings listed above:

Ahistorical Process

MRI

Fisch, R., Weakland, J., & Segal, L. (1982). *The tactics of change.* San Francisco: Jossey-Bass.

Watzlawick, P. (1978). *The language of change: Elements of therapeutic communication.* New York: Basic Books.

Strategic

Haley, J. (1973). *Uncommon therapy: The psychiatric techniques of Milton H. Erickson, M.D.* New York: W.W. Norton.

Haley, J. (1980). *Leaving home.* New York: McGraw Hill.

Haley, J. (1986). *The power tactics of Jesus Christ* (2nd ed.). Rockville, MD: Triangle Press.

Madanes, C. (1981). *Strategic family therapy.* San Francisco: Jossey-Bass.

Madanes, C. (1984). *Behind the one-way mirror: Advances in the practice of strategic therapy.* San Francisco: Jossey-Bass.

Milan

Selvini-Palazzoli, M. (Ed.). (1988). *The work of Mara Selvini-Palazzoli.* Northvale, NJ: Jason Aronson.

Selvini-Palazzoli, M., Cirillo, S., Selvini, M., & Sorrentino, A.M. (1989). *Family games: General models of psychotic processes in the family.* New York: W.W. Norton.

Structural

Minuchin, S. (1974). *Families and family therapy.* Cambridge, MA: Harvard University Press.

Minuchin, S., & Fishman, H.C. (1981). *Family therapy techniques.* Cambridge, MA: Harvard University Press.

Minuchin, S., Montalvo, B., Guerney, B.G., Rosman, B.L., & Schumer, F. (1967). *Families of the slums: An exploration of their structure and treatment.* New York: Basic Books.

Behavioral

Falloon, I.R.H. (Ed.). (1988). *Handbook of behavioral family therapy.* New York: Guilford Press.

Patterson, G. R. (1971). *Families: Applications of social learning to family life.* Champaign, IL: Research Press.

Patterson, G. R. (1982). *Coercive family process.* Eugene, OR: Castalia.

Functional

Alexander, J., & Parsons, B. (1982). *Functional family therapy.* Monterey, CA: Brooks/Cole.

Psychoeducational

Anderson, C.M., Reiss, D.J., & Hogarty, G.E. (1986). *Schizophrenia and the family.* New York: Guilford Press.

Intergenerational

Bowen

Bowen, M. (1978). *Family therapy in clinical practice.* New York: Jason Aronson.

Kerr, M.E., & Bowen, M. (1988). *Family evaluation: An approach based on Bowen theory.* New York: W. W. Norton.

Framo

Framo, J.L. (1982). *Explorations in family and marital therapy: Selected papers of James L. Framo.* New York: Springer Publishing.

Boszormenyi-Nagy

Boszormenyi-Nagy, L. (1987). *Foundations of contextual therapy: Collected papers of Ivan Boszormenyi-Nagy.* New York: Brunner/Mazel.

Boszormenyi-Nagy, L., & Spark, G. (1973). *Invisible loyalties.* New York: Brunner/Mazel.

Object Relations

Kirschner, D., & Kirschner, S. (1986). *Comprehensive family therapy: An integration of systemic and psychodynamic treatment models*. New York: Brunner/Mazel.

Scharff, D.E., & Scharff, J.S. (1987). *Object relations family therapy*. Northvale, NJ: Jason Aronson.

Experiential

Whitaker

Whitaker, C.A., & Bumberry, W.M. (1988). *Dancing with the family: A symbolic-experiential approach*. New York: Brunner/Mazel.

Whitaker, C.A., & Malone, T.P. (1953). *The roots of psychotherapy*. New York: Blakiston.

Satir

Satir, V. (1972). *Peoplemaking*. Palo Alto, CA: Science and Behavior Books.

Satir, V. (1983). *Conjoint family therapy* (3rd. ed.). Palo Alto, CA: Science and Behavior Books.

Satir, V., & Baldwin, M. (1983). *Satir step by step: A guide to creating change in families*. Palo Alto, CA: Science and Behavior Books.

General—Comparative

Fish, L.S. (1989). Comparing structural, strategic, and feminist-informed family therapies: Two delphi studies. *The American Journal of Family Therapy, 17,* 303–314.

Fish, L.S., & Piercy, F.P. (1987). The theory and practice of structural and strategic family therapies: A delphi study. *Journal of Marital and Family Therapy, 13,* 113–125.

MacKinnon, L. (1983). Contrasting strategic and Milan therapies. *Family Process, 22,* 425–441.

Madanes, C., & Haley, J. (1977). Dimensions of family therapy. *The Journal of Nervous and Mental Disease, 165,* 88–98.

Sluzki, C. E. (1983). Process, structure and world views: Toward an integrated view of systemic models in family therapy. *Family Process, 22,* 469–476.

Sluzki, C. E. (1987). Family process: Mapping the journey over 25 years. *Family Process, 26,* 149–153.

ADVANCED: ISSUES AND CONTROVERSIES

Bagarozzi, D., & Anderson, S. (1989). *Personal, marital and family myths: Theoretical formulations and clinical strategies.* New York: W. W. Norton.

Fisher, S., & Greenberg, R.P. (1989). *The limits of biological treatments for psychological distress: Comparisons with psychotherapy and placebo.* Hillsdale, NJ: Erlbaum.

Haley, J. (1984). Marriage or family therapy? *American Journal of Family Therapy, 12,* 3–14.

Haley, J. (1975). Why a mental health clinic should avoid family therapy. *Journal of Marriage and Family Counseling,* Jan., 3–13.

Minuchin, S. (1979). Constructing a therapeutic reality. In E. Kaufman and P. Kaufmann (Eds.), *Family therapy of drug and alcohol abuse* (pp. 3–18). New York: Gardner Press.

Montalvo, B., & Haley, J. (1973). In defense of child therapy. *Family Process, 12*(3), 227–244.

Reiss, D. (1981). *The family's construction of reality.* Cambridge, MA: Harvard University Press.

Sluzki, C.E. (1983). How to stake a territory in the field of family therapy in three easy lessons. *Journal of Marital and Family Therapy, 9,* 235–238.

Torrey, E.F. (1974). *The death of psychiatry.* Radnor, PA: Chilton.

Torrey, E.F. (1986). *Witchdoctors and psychiatrists: The common roots of psychotherapy and its future.* Northvale, NJ: Jason Aronson.

Watzlawick, P. (1984). *The invented reality.* New York: W. W. Norton.

Metaphor and the Use of Story

Gordon, D. (1978). *Therapeutic metaphors.* Cupertino, CA: Meta Publications

Kopp, S. (1971). *Guru: Metaphors from a psychotherapist.* Palo Alto: Science and Behavior Books.

Rosen, S. (1982). *My voice will go with you: The teaching tales of Milton H. Erickson.* New York: W.W. Norton.

Zeig, J. (1980). *A teaching seminar with Milton H. Erickson.* New York: Brunner/Mazel.

FAMILY PROCESSES & PSYCHOPATHOLOGY

Jacob, T. (1987). *Family interaction and psychopathology: Theories, methods, and findings.* New York: Plenum.
Patterson, G.R. (1982). *Coercive Family Process.* Eugene, OR: Castalia.

Behavior as Disease

Breggin, P.R. (1991). *Toxic psychiatry.* New York: St. Martin's Press.
Fisher, S., & Greenberg, R.P. (1985). *The scientific credibility of Freud's theories and therapy.* New York: Columbia University Press.
Kaminer, W. (1992). *I'm dysfunctional, you're dysfunctional: The recovery movement and other self-help fashions.* Reading, MA: Addison-Wesley.
McGuinness, D. (1989). Attention deficit disorder: The emperor's clothes, animal "pharm," and other fiction. In S. Fisher & R.P. Greenberg (Eds.), *The limits of biological treatments for psychological distress: Comparisons with psychotherapy and placebo* (pp. 151–189). Hillsdale, NJ: Erlbaum.
Peele, S. (1989). *Diseasing of America: Addiction treatment out of control.* Lexington, MA: Lexington Books.
Pittman, F. (1992). It's not my fault. *Family Therapy Networker,* Jan./Feb., 57–63.
Szasz, T. (1983). Objections to psychiatry. In J. Miller (Ed.), *States of mind* (pp. 270–290). New York: Pantheon.
Watzlawick, P. (1984). Self-fulfilling prophecies. In P. Watzlawick (Ed.), *The invented reality* (pp. 95–117). New York: W.W. Norton.

Families and Schizophrenia

Breggin, P.R. (1991). *Toxic psychiatry.* New York: St. Martin's Press.
Gottesman, I. I. (1991). *Schizophrenia genesis: The origin of madness.* New York: W. H. Freeman.
Hooley, J. M. (1985). Expressed emotion: A review of the critical literature. *Clinical Psychology Review,* 5, 119–139.

Lewontin, R., Rose, S., & Kamin, L. (1984). *Not in our genes*. New York: Pantheon.

Marital Dyad

Fincham, F., & Bradbury, T.N. (1990). *The psychology of marriage: Basic issues and applications*. New York: Guilford Press.
Gottman, J.M. (1982). Temporal form: Toward a new language for describing relationships. *Journal of Marriage & the Family, 44,* 943–962.

Marital Dyad—Affect Expression

Gottman, J.M., & Levenson, R.W. (1986). Assessing the role of emotion in marriage. *Behavioral Assessment, 8,* 31–48.
Gottman, J.M., & Levenson, R.W. (1988). The social psychophysiology of marriage. In P. Noller & M. A. Fitzpatrick (Eds.), *Perspectives on marital interaction* (pp. 182–200). San Diego, CA: College Hill Press.
Gottman, J.M. (1990). How marriages change. In G.R. Patterson (Ed.), *Family social interaction: Content and methodological issues in the study of aggression and depression* (pp.75–101). Hillsdale, NJ: Erlbaum.
Griffin, W. A. (1993). Transitions from negative affect during marital interaction: Husband and wife differences. *Journal of Family Psychology, 6, 3,* 230–244.

Marital Dyad—Distress

Gottman, J.M. (1979). *Marital interaction: Empirical investigations.* New York: Academic Press.
Schaap, C. (1984). A comparison of the interaction of distressed and nondistressed married couples in a laboratory situation: Literature survey, methodological issues, and an empirical investigation. In K. Hahlweg & N. S. Jacobson (Eds.), *Marital interaction: Analysis and modification* (pp. 133–158). New York: Guilford Press.
Weiss, R.L., & Heyman, R. (1990). Observation of marital interaction. In F.D. Fincham & T.N. Bradbury (Eds.), *The psychology of marriage* (pp. 87–117). New York: Guilford Press.

Interparental Conflict and Behavior Problems in Children

Depner, C.E., Leino, E.V., & Chun, A. (1992). Interparental conflict and child adjustment: A decade review and meta analysis. *Family and Conciliation Courts Review, 30*(3), 323–341.

Emery, R. (1982). Interparental conflict and the children of discord and divorce. *Psychological Bulletin, 92*(2), 310–330.

Forehand, R., Wierson, M., McCombs, A., Brody, G., & Fauber R. (1989). Interparental conflict and adolescent problem behavior: An examination of mechanisms. *Behavior Research Therapy, 27*(4), 365–371.

Wahler, R. & Dumas, J. (1989). Attentional problems in dysfunctional mother-child interactions. *Psychological Bulletin, 105*(1), 116–130.

Substance Abuse

Fingarette, H. (1988). *Heavy drinking: The myth of alcoholism as a disease.* Berkeley: University of California Press.

Gondoli, D. & Jacob, T. (in press). Family treatment of alcoholism. In R. R. Watson (Ed.), *Alcohol and drug abuse reviews: Prevention and treatment of drug and alcohol abuse.* Clifton, NJ: Humana Press.

Kaufman, E., & Kaufmann, P. (1979). *Family therapy of drug and alcohol abuse.* New York: Gardner Press.

Miller, W.R., & Hester, R.K. (1986). Inpatient alcohol treatment: Who benefits? *American Psychologist, 41*(7), 794–805.

Peele, S. (1986) The implications and limitations of genetic models of alcoholism and other addictions. *Journal of Studies of Alcohol, 47*(1), 63–73.

Searles, J.S. (1988). The role of genetics in the pathogenesis of alcoholism. *Journal of Abnormal Psychology, 97*(2), 153–167.

Seilhamer, R.A., & Jacob, T. (in press). Family factors and adjustment of children of alcoholics. In M. Windle & J.S. Searles (Eds.), *Children of alcoholics: A critical review of the literature.* New York: Guilford Press.

Steinglass, P., Bennett, L., Wolin, S., & Reiss, D. (1987). *The alcoholic family.* New York: Basic Books.

Abusive Families

Berger, A. (1985). Characteristics of abusing families. In L. L'Abate, (Ed.), *Handbook of family psychology and therapy* (pp. 900–936). Homewood, IL: Dorsey Press.

Garbarino, J., & Gilliam, G. (1978). *Understanding abusive families.* Lexington, MA.: Lexington Books.

Kempe, C.H., & Kempe, R.S. (1978). *Child abuse.* Cambridge, MA: Harvard University Press.

O'Leary, D., & Vivian, D. (1990). Physical aggression in marriage. In F.D. Fincham & T.N. Bradbury (Eds.), *The psychology of marriage* (pp. 323–348). New York: Guilford Press.

Parke, R.D., & Lewis, N.G. (1983). The family in context: A multilevel interactional analysis of child abuse. In R. Henderson (Ed.), *Parent-child interaction: Theory, research and prospects* (pp. 169–204). New York: Academic Press.

Widom, C.S. (1989). The cycle of violence. *Science, 244*, 160–166.

Children's Adjustment to Divorce

Allison, P., & Furstenberg, F. (1989). How marital dissolution affects children: Variation by age and sex. *Developmental Psychology, 25*(4), 540–549.

Amato, P.R., & Keith, B. (1991). Parental divorce and the well being of children: A meta analysis. *Psychological Bulletin, 110*(1), 26–46.

Chase-Lansdale, L., & Hetherington, M. (1990). The impact of divorce on life-span development: Short and longterm effects. In P.B. Baltes, D.L. Featherman, & R.M. Lerner (Eds.), *Life-span development and behavior* (Vol. 10, pp. 105–151). Hillsdale, NJ: Erlbaum.

Hetherington, M., Stanely-Hagan, M., & Anderson, E. (1989). Marital Transitions: A child's perspective. *American Psychologist, 44*(2), 303–312.

Wolchik, S., Ramirez, R., Sandler, I., Fisher, J., Balls, P., & Brown, C. (1990). *Inner-city, poor children of divorce: Negative divorce-related events, problematic beliefs, and adjustment problems.* New York: Gardner Press.

OBSERVATIONAL METHODOLOGY

Patterson, G.R., & Reid, J.B. (1984). Social interaction processes within the family: The study of the moment by moment family transactions in which human social development is embedded. *Journal of Applied Developmental Psychology, 5,* 237–262.

Weiss, R.L. (1989). The circle of voyeurs: Observing the observers of marital and family interactions. *Behavioral Assessement, 11,* 135–148.

Weiss, R.L., & Heyman, R. (1990). Observation of marital interaction. In F.D. Fincham & T.N. Bradbury (Eds.), *The psychology of marriage* (pp. 87–117). New York: Guilford Press.

Analysis of Marital and Family Interaction

Bakeman, R., & Gottman, J.M. (1980). *Observing Interaction : An introduction to sequential analysis.* New York: Cambridge University Press.

Gardner, W., & Griffin, W.A. (1989). Methods for the analysis of parallel streams of continuously recorded social behaviors. *Psychological Bulletin, 105*(3), 446–455.

Griffin, W.A. (1993a). Event history analysis of of marital and family interaction: A practical introduction. *Journal of Family Psychology, 6,*(3), 211–229.

Griffin, W.A., & Gardner, W. (1989). Analysis of behavioral durations in observational studies of social interactio *Psychological Bulletin,106* (3,) 497–502.

Griffin, W.A. & Gottman, J.M. (1990). Statistical methods for analyzing family interaction. In G.R. Patterson (Ed.), *Family social interaction: Content and methodology issues in the study of aggression and depression* (pp. 130–168). Hillsdale, NJ: Erblaum.

Suen, H.,Ary, D. (1989). *Analyzing quantitative behavioral observation data.* Hillsdale, NJ: Erlbaum.

MARRIAGE AND FAMILY THERAPY RESEARCH

Issues

Liddle, H. (1991b). Empirical values and the culture of family therapy. *Journal of Marriage and Family Therapy*, *17*, 4, 327–348.

Outcome

Baucom, D., & Hoffman, J. (1986). The effectiveness of marital therapy: Current status and application to the clinical setting. In N. Jacobson & A. Gurman (Eds.), *Clinical handbook of marital therapy* (pp. 597–620). New York: Guilford Press.

Beach, S., & O'Leary, D. (1985). Current status of outcome research in marital therapy. In L. L'Abate (Ed.), *The handbook of family psychology and therapy*. Homewood, IL: Dorsey.

Gurman, A.S., & Kniskern, D.P., & Pinsof, W.M. (1986). Research on the process and outcome of marital and family therapy. In S.L. Garfield & A.E. Bergin (Eds.), *Handbook of psychotherapy and behavior change* (3rd ed., pp. 565–622). New York: Wiley.

Hazelrigg, M.D., Cooper, H.M., & Bourdin, C.M. (1987). Evaluating the effectiveness of family therapies: An integrative review and analysis. *Psychological Bulletin*, *101*, 428–442.

Wynne, L. (1988). *The state of the art in family therapy research*. New York: W.W. Norton.

A SAMPLING OF RELEVANT JOURNALS

Marriage and Family Therapy Journals

Refereed

American Journal of Family Therapy
Family Process
Journal of Family Psychology
Journal of Family Therapy
Journal of Marriage and Family Therapy

Nonrefereed (nonacademic format)
Family Therapy Networker
Journal of Strategic and Systemic Therapies

Other Relevant Clinical and Child Development Journals

Behavioral Assessment
Child Development
Developmental Psychology
Family Relations
Journal of Consulting & Clinical Psychology
Journal of Marriage and the Family
Journal of Personality & Social Psychology
Psychological Bulletin (excellent review articles)

Newsletters

AFTA Newsletter (AFTA)
Family Therapy News (AAMFT)

WHAT TO AVOID

Lay Books

Avoid books that promote simple answers to complex issues (e.g., "Improve your marriage in 10 days.")
Avoid books that have catchy or provocative titles (e.g., "Sixty and sexy")
Avoid books that promote disease and irresponsibility (e.g., addiction, codependency).

References

Ackerman, N. (1958). *The psychodynamics of family life.* New York: Basic Books.

Ackerman, N. (1966). *Treating the troubled family.* New York: Basic Books.

Alexander, J. F. (1988). Phases of family therapy process: A framework for clinicians and researchers. In L. C. Wynne (Ed.), *The state of the art in family therapy research: Controversies and recommendations* (pp. 175–188). New York: Family Process Press.

Alexander, J.F., Barton, C., Schiavo, R.S., & Parsons, B. V. (1977). Systems-behavioral intervention with families of delinquents: Therapist characteristics, family behavior, and outcome. *Journal of Consulting and Clinical Psychology, 44,* 656–664.

American Psychiatric Association. (1975). *A psychiatric glossary* (4th ed.). New York: Basic Books.

Anderson, C.M., & Stewart, S. (1983). *Mastering resistance: A practical guide to family therapy.* New York: Guilford Press.

Anderson, C.M., & Reiss, D.J., & Hogarty, G.E. (1986). *Schizophrenia and the family.* New York: Guilford Press.

Aponte, H. J., & VanDeusen, J. M. (1981). Structural family therapy. In A.S. Gurman & D.P. Kniskern (Eds.), *Handbook of family therapy,* Vol. I (pp. 310–360). New York: Brunner/Mazel.

Ashby, W.R. (1956). *An introduction to cybernetics.* London: Methuen.

Attneave, F. (1956). *Applications of information theory to psychology.* New York: Holt, Rinehart & Winston.

Azrin, N. H., Naster, J. B., & Jones, R. (1973). Reciprocity counseling: A rapid learning based procedure for marital counseling. *Behavior Research and Therapy, 11,* 365–383.

Bagarozzi, D., & Anderson, S. (1989). *Personal, marital and family myths: Theoretical formulations and clinical strategies.* New York: W. W. Norton.

Bandura, A. (1978). The self-system in reciprocal determinism. *American Psychologist, 33,* 344–358.

Barker, P. (1985). *Using metaphors in psychotherapy.* New York: Brunner/Mazel.

Barton, C., & Alexander, J.F. (1981). Functional family therapy. In A.S. Gurman & D.P. Kniskern (Eds.), *The handbook of family therapy,* Vol. I (pp. 403–443). New York: Brunner/Mazel.

Bateson, G. (1972). *Steps to an ecology of mind.* New York: Ballantine.

Bateson, G. (1979). *Mind and nature.* New York: E.P. Dutton.

Bateson, G., Jackson, D.D., Haley, J., & Weakland, J. (1956). Toward a theory of schizophrenia. *Behavioral Science, 1,* 251–264.

Baucom, D., & Epstein, N. (1990). *Cognitive-behavioral marital therapy.* New York: Brunner/Mazel.

Beck, A. (1976). *Cognitive therapy and the emotional disorders.* New York: International University Press.

Befera, M.S., & Barkley, R.A. (1985). Hyperactive and normal girls and boys: Mother-child interaction, parent psychiatric status and child psychopathology. *Journal of Child Psychology and Psychiatry, 26,* 439–452.

Belsky, J., & Pensky, E. (1988). Developmental history, personality, and family relationships: Toward an emergent family system. In R. A. Hinde & J. Stevenson-Hinde (Eds.), *Relationships within families: Mutual influences* (pp. 193–217). Oxford: Clarendon Press.

Birdwhistell, R.L. (1952). *Introduction to kinesics.* Louisville, KY: University of Louisville Press.

Bodin, A. (1981). The interactional view: Family therapy approaches of the Mental Research Institute. In A.S. Gurman & D.P. Kniskern (Eds.), *Handbook of family therapy,* Vol. I (pp. 267–309). New York: Brunner/Mazel.

Boscolo, L., Cecchin, G., Hoffman, L., & Penn, P. (1987). *Milan systemic family therapy.* New York: Basic Books.

Boszormenyi-Nagy, I. (1987). *Foundations of contextual therapy:*

    Collected papers of Ivan Boszormenyi-Nagy, M. D. New York:
    Brunner/Mazel.

Boszormenyi-Nagy, I., & Spark, G. (1973). *Invisible loyalties.*
    Hagerstown, MD: Harper & Row.

Boszormenyi-Nagy, I., & Ulrich, D.N. (1981). Contextual family ther-
    apy. In A.S. Gurman & D.P. Kniskern (Eds.), *Handbook of family
    therapy,* Vol. I (pp. 159-186). New York: Brunner/Mazel.

Bowen, M. (1976). Theory in the practice of psychotherapy. In P.J.
    Guerin (Ed.), *Family therapy: Theory and practice.* New York:
    Gardner Press.

Bowen, M. (1978). *Family therapy in clinical practice.* New York:
    Jason Aronson.

Bowlby, J. (1969). *Attachment and loss.* Vol. I: *Attachment.* New York:
    Basic Books.

Bowlby, J. (1973). *Attachment and loss.* Vol. II: *Separation.* New York:
    Basic Books.

Breggin, P.R. (1991). *Toxic psychiatry.* New York: St. Martin's Press.

Broderick, C.B., & Schrador, S.S. (1001). The history of professional
    marriage and family therapy. In A.S. Gurman & D.P. Kniskern
    (Eds.), *Handbook of family therapy,* Vol. II (pp. 3—40). New York:
    Brunner/Mazel.

Buckley, W. (1967). *Sociology and modern systems theory.* Englewood
    Cliffs, NJ: Prentice-Hall.

Burbatti, G. L., & Formenti, L. (1988). *The Milan approach to family
    therapy* (E. Cosmo, Trans.). Northvale, NJ: Jason Aronson.

Carter, E., & McGoldrick, M. (1988). *The changing family life cycle: A
    framework for family therapy (2nd Ed.)* Nedham Heights, MA:
    Allyn and Bacon.

Chase-Lansdale, L., & Hetherington, M. (1990). The impact of divorce
    on life-span development: Short and long term effects. In P. B.
    Baltes, D. L. Featherman & R. M. Lerner (Eds.), *Life-span develop-
    ment and behavior* (Vol. 10, pp. 105–131). Hillsdale, NJ:
    Erlbaum.

Cleghorn, J., & Levin, S. (1973). Training family therapists by setting
    learning objectives. *American Journal of Orthopsychiatry, 43,*
    439–446.

Colapinto, J. (1991). Structural family therapy. In A.S. Gurman &
    D.P. Kniskern (Eds.), *Handbook of family therapy,* Vol. II.
    (pp. 417–443). New York: Brunner/Mazel.

Coles, G.S. (1987). *The learning mystique: A critical look at "Learning Disabilities."* New York: Pantheon.

Crane, D. R., Griffin, W. A., & Hill, R. D. (1986). Influence of therapist skills on client perceptions of marriage and family therapy outcome: Implications for supervision. *Journal of Marriage and Family Therapy, 12*(1), 91–96.

Crane, D., Allgood, S., Larson, J., & Griffin, W. (1990) Assessing marital quality with distressed and non-distressed couples: A comparison and equivalency table for three frequently used measures. *Journal of Marriage and the Family, 52,* 87–93.

Darnell, D.K. (1972). Information theory: An approach to human communication. In R.W. Budd and B.D. Ruben (Eds.), *Approaches to human communication* (pp. 156–169). New York: Spartan.

Davidson, M. (1983). *Uncommon sense.* Los Angeles: J. P. Tarcher.

de Shazer, S. (1984). The death of resistance. *Family Process, 23,* 79–93.

de Shazer, S. (1985). *Keys to solutions in brief therapy.* New York: W.W. Norton.

de Shazer, S. (1988). *Clues: Investigating solutions in brief therapy.* New York W.W. Norton.

Dewan, M.J., & Koss, M. (1989). The clinical impact of the side effects of psychotropic drugs. In S. Fisher & R.P. Greenberg (Eds.), *The limits of biological treatments for psychological distress: Comparisons with psychotherapy and placebo* (pp. 189–234). Hillsdale, NJ: Erlbaum.

Doherty, W. J., & Boss, P. G. (1991). Values and ethics in family therapy. In A. S. Gurman & D. P. Kniskern (Eds.), *Handbook of family therapy,* Vol. II (pp. 607–637). New York: Brunner/Mazel.

Duhl, B. S. (1983). *From the inside out and other metaphors: Creative and integrative approaches to training in systems thinking.* New York: Brunner/Mazel.

Duhl, B. S., & Duhl, F. J. (1981). Integrative family therapy. In A. S. Gurman and D. P. Kniskern (Eds.), *Handbook of family therapy,* Vol. I (pp. 483–516). New York: Brunner/Mazel.

Duhl, F. J., Kantor, D., & Duhl, B. S. (1973). Learning, space, and action in family therapy: A primer of sculpture. In D. A. Bloch (Ed.), *Techniques of family psychotherapy: A primer* (pp. 47–64). New York: Grune & Stratton.

Ekman, P., & Friesen, W. (1984). *Unmasking the face.* Palo Alto: Consulting Psychologists Press.

Ellis, A. (1975). *How to live with a "neutrotic"* (rev. ed.). New York: Crown.

Emery, R. (1982). Interparental conflict and the children of discord and divorce. *Psychological Bulletin, 92*(2), 310–330.

Erskine, R. (1991). Transactional analysis and family therapy. In A. M. Horne & J. L Passmore (Eds.), *Family counseling and therapy* (pp. 497–527). Itasca, IL: Peacock.

Eshleman, J.R. (1988). *The family: An introduction* (5th ed.). Boston: Allyn & Bacon.

Falloon, I.R.H. (1985). *Family management of schizophrenia: A study of the clinical, social, family and economic benefits.* Baltimore: Johns Hopkins University Press.

Falloon, I.R.H. (Ed.). (1988). *Handbook of behavioral family therapy.* New York: Guilford Press.

Falloon, I.R.H. (1991). Behavioral family therapy. In A.S. Gurman & D.P. Kniskern (Eds.), *Handbook of family therapy,* Vol. II (pp. 65–95). New York: Brunner/Mazel.

Falloon, I.R.H., Boyd, J.L., & McGill, C.W. (Eds.). (1984). *Family care of schizophrenia.* New York: Guilford Press.

Falloon, I.R.H., & Lillie, F.J. (1988). Behavioral family therapy: An overview. In I.R.H. Falloon (Ed.), *The handbook of behavioral family therapy.* New York: Guilford Press.

Fenichel, O. (1945). *The psychoanalytic theory of neurosis.* New York: W.W. Norton.

Fincham, F., & Bradbury, T. N. (1990). *The psychology of marriage: Basic issues and applications.* New York: Guilford Press.

Fisch, R., Weakland, J., & Segal, L. (1982). *The tactics of change.* San Francisco: Jossey-Bass.

Fisher, S., & Greenberg, R.P. (1985). *The scientific credibility of Freud's theories and therapy.* New York: Columbia University Press.

Fishman, H.C. (1988). *Treating troubled adolescents.* New York: Basic Books.

Fleuridas, C., Nelson, T.S., & Rosenthal, D.M. (1986). The evolution of circular questions: Training family therapists. *Journal of Marital and Family Therapy, 25,* 120–125.

Fogarty, T.F. (1976a). On emptiness and closeness: Part I. *The Family, 3*(1), 3–10.

Fogarty, T.F. (1976b). On emptiness and closeness: Part II. *The Family,* 3(2), 37–49.

Foley, V.D. (1974). *An introduction to family therapy.* New York: Grune & Stratton.

Framo, J.L. (1982). *Explorations in family and marital therapy: Selected papers of James L. Framo.* New York: Springer Publishing.

Furstenberg, F. F., & Seltzer, J. A. (1986). Divorce and child development. In *Sociological studies of child development,* Vol. 1 (pp. 137–160). Greenwich, CT: JAI Press.

Gelles, R.J., & Straus, M.A. (1987). Is violence towards children increasing? A comparison of 1975 and 1985 national survey rates. *Journal of Interpersonal Violence, 2,* 212–222.

Gondoli, D., & Jacob, T. (in press). Family treatment of alcoholism. In R. R. Watson (Ed.), *Alcohol and drug abuse reviews: Prevention and treatment of drug and alcohol abuse.* Clifton, NJ: Humana Press.

Gordon, S.B., & Davidson, N. (1981). Behavioral parent training. In A.S. Gurman & D.P. Kniskern (Eds.), *Handbook of family therapy,* Vol. I (pp. 517–555). New York: Brunner/Mazel.

Gottesman, I. I. (1991). *Schizophrenia genesis: The origin of madness.* New York: W. H. Freeman & Company.

Gray, W., Duhl, F. J., & Rizzo, N. D. (1969). *General systems theory and psychiatry.* Boston: Little, Brown.

Greenberg, G. S. (1977). The family interactional perspective: A study and examination of the work of Don D. Jackson. *Family Process, 16,* 385–412.

Griffin, W.A., & Greene, S.M. (in press). Social interaction and symptom sequences: A case study of orofacial bradykinesia exacerbation in Parkinson's disease during negative marital interaction. *Psychiatry.*

Griffin, W.A., & Morgan, A. (1988). Conflict in maritally distressed military couples. *American Journal of Family Therapy, 16,* 14–22.

Grych, J.H., & Fincham, F.D. (1990). Marital conflict and children's adjustment: A cognitive-contextual framework. *Psychological Bulletin, 108(2),* 267–290.

Guerin, P.J. (1976). Family therapy: The first twenty-five years. In P.J. Guerin (Ed.), *Family therapy: Theory and practice* (pp. 2–22). New York: Gardner Press.

Guerin, P.J., Fay, L., Burden, S.L., & Kauggo, J.G. (1987). *The evaluation and treatment of marital conflict.* New York: Basic Books.

Gurman, A.S., & Kniskern, D.P., & Pinsof, W.M. (1986). Research on the process and outcome of marital and family therapy. In S.L. Garfield & A.E. Bergin (Eds.), *Handbook of psychotherapy and behavior change* (3rd ed., pp. 565–622). New York: Wiley.

Haley, J. (1963). *Strategies of psychotherapy.* New York: Grune and Stratton.

Haley, J. (1973). Uncommon therapy: The psychiatric techniques of Milton H. Erickson, M.D. New York: W.W. Norton.

Haley, J. (1976). Problems in training therapists. In J. Haley (Ed.), *Problem solving therapy.* San Francisco: Jossey-Bass.

Haley, J. (1980). *Leaving home.* New York: McGraw Hill.

Haley, J. (1981). *Reflections of therapy and other essays.* Chevy Chase, MD: The Family Institute of Washington, D.C.

Haley, J. (1984). Ordeal therapy: Unusual ways to change behavior San Francisco: Jossey-Bass.

Haley, J. (1987). *Problem-solving therapy for effective family therapy* (2nd ed.). San Francisco: Jossey-Bass.

Haley, J. (1988). Reflections on therapy supervision. In H. Liddle, D. Breunlin, & R. Schwartz (Eds.), *Handbook of family therapy training and supervision.* New York: Guilford Press.

Haley, J., & Hoffman, L. (1967). *Techniques of family therapy.* New York: Basic Books.

Hoffman, L. (1981). *Foundation of family therapy.* New York: Basic Books.

Hoffman, L. (1988). The family life cycle and discontinuous change. In B. Carter & M. McGoldrick (Eds.), *The changing family life cycle* (2nd ed.). New York: Gardner Press.

Hoffman, L. (1990). Constructing realities: An art of lenses. *Family Process, 20, 11.*

Holtzworth-Munroe, A., & Jacobson, N. (1991). Behavioral marital therapy. In A.S. Gurman & D.P. Kniskern (Eds.), *Handbook of family therapy,* Vol. II (pp. 96–133). New York: Brunner/Mazel.

Holzman, P. S. (1970). *Psychoanalysis and psychopathology.* New York: McGraw-Hill.

Hooley, J. M. (1985). Expressed emotion: A review of the critical literature. *Clinical Psychology Review, 5, 119–139.*

Hops, H., Sherman, L., & Biglan, A. (1990). Maternal depression, marital discord, and children's behavior: A developmental perspective. In G.R. Patterson (Ed.) *Family social interaction: Content and methodology issues in the study of aggression and depression* (pp. 185–208). Hillsdale, NJ: Erlbaum.

Imber-Black, E., Roberts, J., & Whiting, R. (1989). *Rituals in families and family therapy.* New York: W.W. Norton.

Jackson, D. D. (1960). *The etiology of schizophrenia.* New York: Basic Books.

Jackson, D. D. (1964). *Myths of madness.* New York: Macmillan.

Jacobson, N.S., & Margolin, G. (1979). *Marital therapy: Strategies based on social learning and behavior exchange principles.* New York: Brunner/Mazel.

Kaminer, W. (1992). *I'm dysfunctional, you're dysfunctional.* New York: Addison-Wesley.

Kazdin, A. B. (1987). Treatment of antisocial behavior in children: Current status and future directions. *Psychological Bulletin, 102,* 187–203.

Klein, M. (1948). *Contributions to psychoanalysis.* London: Hogarth Press.

Kempler, W. (1991). Gestalt family therapy. In A. M. Horne & J. L Passmore (Eds.), *Family counseling and therapy* (pp. 263– 300). Itasca, IL: Peacock.

Kernberg, O. (1975). *Borderline conditions and pathological narcissim.* New York: Jason Aronson.

Kernberg, O. (1976). *Object-relations theory and clinical psychoanalysis.* New York: Jason Aronson.

Kerr, M. E., & Bowen, M. (1988). *Family evaluation: An approach based on Bowen theory.* New York: W. W. Norton.

Kerr, M. E. (1981). Family systems theory and therapy. In A.S. Gurman & D.P. Kniskern (Eds.), *Handbook of family therapy,* Vol. I (pp. 226–264). New York: Brunner/Mazel.

Kirschner, D. A., & Kirschner, S. (1986). *Comprehensive family therapy: An integration of systemic and psychodynamic treatment models.* New York: Brunner/Mazel.

Konner, M. (1982). *The tangled wing: Biological constraints on the human spirit.* New York: Holt, Rinehart & Winston.

Kopp, S. (1971). *Guru: Metaphors from a psychotherapist.* Palo Alto: Science and Behavior Books.

L'Abate, L. Ganahl, G., & Hansen, J. C. (1986). *Methods in family therapy*. Englewood Cliffs, NJ: Prentice-Hall.

Laing, R.D. (1960). *The divided self*. London: Tavistock Publications.

Laing, R.D. (1960). Mystification, confusion, and conflict. In I. Boszormenyi-Nagy & J.L. Framo (Eds.), *Intensive family therapy*. New York: Harper and Row.

Lamb, M.E., Thompson, R.A., Gardner, W., Charnov, E.L., & Estes, D. (1984). Security of infantile attachment as assessed in the "Strange Situation": Its study and biological interpretation. *Behavioral and Brain Sciences, 7*, 127–147.

Lamb, M.E., Thompson, R.A., Gardner, W., & Charnov, E.L. (1985). *Infant-mother attachment: The origins and developmental significance of individual differences in Strange Situation behavior*. Hillsdale, NJ: Erlbaum.

Leff, J., & Vaughn, C. (1985). *Expressed emotion in families: Its significance for mental illness*. New York: Guilford Press.

Levant, R. (1984). *Family therapy: A comparative overview*. Englewood Cliffs, NJ: Prentice-Hall.

Lowontin, R., Rose, S., & Kamin, L. (1984). *Not in our genes*. New York: Pantheon.

Liddle, H. (1988). Systemic supervision: Conceptual overlays and pragmatic guidelines. In H. Liddle, D. Breunlin, & R. Schwartz (Eds.), *Handbook of family therapy training and supervision*. New York: Guilford Press.

Liddle, H. (1991a). Training and supervision in family therapy: A comprehensive and critical analysis. In A.S. Gurman & D.P. Kniskern (Eds.), *Handbook of family therapy*, Vol. II. (pp. 638–697). New York: Brunner/Mazel.

Liddle, H. (1991b). Empirical values and the culture of family therapy. *Journal of Marriage and Family Therapy, 17*, 4, 327–348.

Liddle, H., Breunlin, D., & Schwartz, R. (Eds.). (1988). *Handbook of family therapy training and supervision*. New York: Guilford Press.

Lidz, T., Cornelison, A., & Fleck, S. (1965). *Schizophrenia and the family*. New York: International Universities Press.

Lidz, T., Cornelison, A., Fleck, S., & Terry, D. (1957). Intrafamilial environment of the schizphrenic patient. I: The father. *Psychiatry, 20*, 329–342.

Lidz, T., & Fleck, S. (1960). Schizophrenia, human integration, and the role of the family. In D.D. Jackson (Ed.), *The etiology of schizo-phrenia*. New York: Basic Books.

Madanes, C. (1981). *Strategic family therapy*. San Francisco: Jossey-Bass.

Madanes, C. (1984). *Behind the one-way mirror: Advances in the practice of strategic therapy*. San Francisco: Jossey-Bass.

Madanes, C. (1991). Strategic family therapy. In A. S. Gurman & D. P. Kniskern (Eds.), *Handbook of family therapy*, Vol. II (pp. 396–416). New York: Brunner/Mazel.

Mahler, M., Pine, F., & Bergman, A. (1975). *The psychological birth of the human infant*. New York: Basic Books.

Maruyama, M. (1963). The second cybernetics: Deviation-amplifying mutual causal processes. *American Scientist, 51*, 164–179.

Maturana, H., & Varela, F. (1987). *The tree of knowledge: The biological roots of human understanding*. Boston: Shambhala.

McFarlane, W.R. (1991). Family psychoeducational treatment. In A.S. Gurman & D.P. Kniskern (Eds.), *Handbook of family therapy*, Vol. II (pp. 363-395). New York: Brunner/Mazel.

McGoldrick, M., & Gerson, R. (1985). *Genograms in family assessment*. New York: W. W. Norton.

McGuinness, D. (1989). Attention deficit disorder: The emperor's clothes, animal "pharm," and other fiction. In S. Fisher & R.P. Greenberg (Eds.), *The limits of biological treatments for psychological distress: Comparisons with psychotherapy and placebo* (pp. 151–189). Hillsdale, NJ: Erlbaum.

Melamed, B.G., & Brenner, G. F. (1990). Social support and chronic medical stress: An interaction-based approach. *Journal of Social and Clinical Psychology, 9*, 104–117.

Minuchin, S. (1974). *Families and family therapy*. Cambridge, MA: Harvard University Press.

Minuchin, S. (1979). Constructing a Therapeutic Reality. In E. Kaufman and P. Kaufmann (Eds.), *Family therapy of drug and alcohol abuse* (pp. 3–18). New York: Gardner Press.

Minuchin, S., & Fishman, H.C. (1981). *Family therapy techniques*. Cambridge, MA: Harvard University Press.

Minuchin, S., Montalvo, B., Guerney, B.G., Rosman, B.L., & Schumer, F. (1967). *Families of the slums: An exploration of their structure and treatment*. New York: Basic Books.

Minuchin, S., Rosman, B.L., & Baker, L. (1978). *Psychosomatic fami-*

lies: Anorexia nervosa in context. Cambridge, MA: Harvard University Press.

Montalvo, B. (1973). Aspects of live supervision. *Family Process, 12,* 343–359.

Montalvo, B., & Haley, J. (1973). In defense of child therapy. *Family Process, 12*(3), 227–244.

Napier, A. Y., & Whitaker, C. A. (1978). *The family crucible.* New York: Harper & Row.

Neill, J.R. & Kniskern, D.P. (Eds.) (1982). *From psyche to system: The evolving therapy of Carl Whitaker.* New York: Guilford Press.

Nichols, M. P. (1987). *The self in the system: Expanding the limits of family therapy.* New York: Brunner/Mazel.

O'Hanlon, W.H. (1987). *Taproots: Underlying principles of Milton Erickson's therapy and hypnosis.* New York: W.W. Norton.

O'Hanlon, W.H., & Weiner-Davis, M. (1989). *In search of solutions: A new direction in psychotherapy.* New York: W.W. Norton.

Papero, D. (1990). *Bowen family systems theory.* Boston: Allyn & Bacon.

Papp, P. (1980). The Greek chorus and other techniques of paradoxical therapy. *Family Process, 19,* 45–57.

Papp, P. (1983). *The process of change.* New York: Guilford Press.

Patterson, G.R. (1971). *Families: Applications of social learning to family life.* Champaign, IL: Research Press.

Patterson, G.R. (1982). *Coercive family process.* Eugene, OR: Castalia.

Patterson, G.R., & Forgatch, M.S. (1985). Therapist behavior as a determinant for client noncompliance: A paradox for the behavior modifier. *Journal of Consulting and Clinical Psychology, 53,* 846–851.

Patterson, G.R., & Forgatch, M.S. (1990). Initiation and maintenance of process disrupting single mother families. In G.R. Patterson (Ed.), *Family social interaction: Content and methodology issues in the study of aggression and depression* (pp. 209–248). Hillsdale, NJ: Erblaum.

Patterson, G.R., & Reid, J.B. (1984). Social interaction processes within the family: The study of the moment by moment transactions in which human social development is embedded. *Journal of Applied Developmental Psychology, 5,* 237–262.

Patterson, G.R., Reid, J.B., & Dishion, T.J. (1992). *Antisocial Boys.* Eugene, OR: Castalia.

Peele, S. (1989). *Diseasing of America: Addiction treatment out of control*. Lexington, MA: Lexington Books.

Penn, P. (1982). Circular questioning. *Family Process, 21,* 263–280.

Penn, P. (1985). Feed-forward: Further questioning, future maps. *Family Process, 24,* 299–310.

Pittman, F. (1992). It's not my fault. *Family Therapy Networker,* Jan./Feb., 57–63.

Plomin, R. (1989). Environment and genes. *American Psychologist,* 44(2), 105–111.

Rabkin, R. (1977). *Strategic psychotherapy.* New York: Basic Books.

Reiss, D. (1981). *The family's construction of reality.* Cambridge, MA: Harvard University Press.

Reiss, D. (1988). Theoretical versus tactical inference: Or, how to do family psychotherapy research without dying of boredom. In L.C. Wynne (Ed.), *The state of the art in family therapy research* (pp. 33–45). New York: Family Process Press.

Riley, S. (1992). Treating the family with an adolescent with family art therapy. In J. D. Atwood (Ed.), *Family therapy* (pp. 123–134). Chicago: Nelson-Hall.

Rutter, M. (1983). Stress, coping, and development: Some issues and some questions. In N. Garmezy & M. Rutter (Eds.), *Stress, coping and development in children* (pp. 1–41). New York: McGraw-Hill.

Rutter, M., Macdonald, H., Le Couteur, A., Harrington, R., Bolton, P., & Bailey, A. (1990). Genetic factors in child psychiatric disorders–II. Empirical findings. *Journal of Child Psychology and Psychiatry,* 31(1), 39–83.

Sanua, V. (1986). The organic etiology of infantile autism: A critical review of the literature. *International Journal of Neuroscience, 30,* 195–225.

Satir, V. (1972). *Peoplemaking.* Palo Alto, CA: Science and Behavior Books.

Satir, V. (1983). *Conjoint family therapy* (3rd. ed.). Palo Alto, CA: Science and Behavior Books.

Satir, V., & Baldwin, M. (1983). *Satir step by step: A guide to creating change in families.* Palo Alto, CA: Science and Behavior Books.

Scarnati, R. (1986). An outline of hazardous side effects of Ritalin (Methylphenidate). *International Journal of Addictions, 21,* 837–41.

Scharff, D. E., & Scharff, J. S. (1987). *Object relations family therapy.* Northvale, NJ: Jason Aronson.

Segal, L. (1991). Brief therapy: The MRI approach. In A. S. Gurman & D. P. Kniskern (Eds.), *Handbook of family therapy,* Vol. II (pp. 171–199). New York: Brunner/Mazel.

Selvini-Palazzoli, M., Boscolo, L., Cecchin, G., & Prata, G. (1978). *Paradox and counterparadox.* New York: Jason Aronson.

Selvini-Palazzoli, M., Cirillo, S., Selvini, M., & Sorrentino, A.M. (1989). *Family games: General models of psychotic processes in the family.* New York: W.W. Norton.

Shannon, C.E., & Weaver, W. (1949). *The mathematical theory of communication.* Urbana: University of Illinois Press.

Skynner, R. (1981). An open systems, group analytic approach to family therapy. In A.S. Gurman & D.P. Kniskern (Eds.), *Handbook of family therapy,* Vol. I (pp. 39–84). New York: Brunner/Mazel.

Stanton, M.D. (1981). Strategic approaches to family therapy. In A.S. Gurman & D.P. Kniskern (Eds.), *Handbook of family therapy,* Vol. I (pp. 361–402) New York: Brunner/Mazel.

Stanton, M.D., & Todd, T., and associates. (1982). *The family therapy of drug abuse and addiction.* New York: Guilford Press.

Steinglass, P. (1987). A systems view of family interaction and psychopathogy. In T. Jacob (Ed.), *Family interaction and psychopathology: Theories, methods, and findings.* New York: Plenum.

Steinglass, P., Bennett, L., Wolin, S., & Reiss, D. (1987). *The alcoholic family.* New York: Basic Books.

Stern, D. (1985). *The interpersonal world of the infant.* New York: Basic Books.

Storm, C.L. & Heath, A. (1985). Model of supervision: Using therapy as a guide. *The Clinical Supervisor, 3,* 87–96.

Straus, M.A. (1974). Leveling, civility, and violence in the family. *Journal of Marriage and the Family, 36,* 13–29.

Straus, M.A., & Gelles, R. (1986). Societal change and family violence from 1975 to 1985 as revealed by two national surveys. *Journal of Marriage and the Family, 41,* 75–88.

Sullivan, H.S. (1953). *The interpersonal theory of psychiatry.* New York: W.W. Norton.

Szasz, T. (1961). *The myth of mental illness.* New York: Harper & Row.

Szasz, T. (1970). *The manufacture of madness: A comparative study of the inquisition and the mental health movement.* New York: Dell.

Szasz, T. (1983). Objections to psychiatry. In J. Miller (Ed.), *States of mind* (pp. 270–290). New York: Pantheon.

Thayer, L. (1991). Toward a person-centered approach to family therapy. In A. M. Horne & J. L. Passmore (Eds.), *Family counseling and therapy* (pp. 301–346). Itasca, IL: Peacock.

Tomm, K. (1984a). One perspective on the Milan systemic approach: Part I. Overview of development, theory, and practice. *Journal of Marital and Family Therapy, 10,* 113–125.

Tomm, K. (1984b). One perspective on the Milan systemic approach: Part II. Description of session format, interviewing style, and interventions. *Journal of Marital and Family Therapy, 10,* 253–271.

Tomm, K. (1985). Circular questioning: A multifaceted clinical tool. In D. Campbell & R. Draper (Eds.), *Application of systemic family therapy: The Milan method* (pp. 33–45). New York: Grune & Stratton.

Tomm, K. (1987). Interventive interviewing, Part I. Strategizing as a fourth guideline for the therapist. *Family Process, 26,* 3–13.

Tomm, K. (1987). Interventive interviewing, Part II. Reflexive questioning as a means top enable self-healing. *Family Process, 26,* 167–184.

Tomm, K. (1988). Interventive interviewing, Part III: Intending to ask linear, circular, strategic, or reflexive questions. *Family Process, 27,* 1–15.

Torgenrud, J., & Storm, C. L. (1989). One-person family therapy? An analysis of family therapy schools. *American Journal of Family Therapy, 17*(2), 143–154.

Torrey, E.F. (1974). *The death of psychiatry.* Radnor, PA: Chilton.

Torrey, E.F. (1986). *Witchdoctors and psychiatrists: The common roots of psychotherapy and its future.* Northvale, NJ: Jason Aronson.

Truax, C.B., & Carkhuff, R.R. (1967). *Toward effective counseling and psychotherapy.* Chicago: Aldine.

von Bertalanffy, L. (1933). *Modern theories of development.* Oxford: Oxford University Press.

von Bertalanffy, L. (1950). An outline of General Systems Theory. *British Journal of the Philosophy of Science, 1,* 134–165.

von Bertalanffy, L. (1966). General system theory and psychiatry. In S. Arieti (Ed.): *The American handbook of psychiatry* (Vol. 3, pp. 702–721). New York: Basic Books.

von Bertalanffy, L. (1968). *General system theory.* New York: George Braziller.

von Bertalanffy, L. (1976). *Robots, men and minds.* New York: Goeorge Braziller.

von Bertalanffy, L. (1981). *A systems view of man.* Boulder, CO: Westview. Edited by LaViolette, P. A.

Wahler, R., & Dumas, J. (1989). Attentional problems in dysfunctional mother-child interactions. *Psychological Bulletin,* 105(1), 116–130.

Watzlawick, P. (1976). *How real is real?* New York: Random House.

Watzlawick, P. (1978). *The language of change: Elements of therapeutic communication.* New York: Basic Books.

Watzlawick, P. (Ed.). (1984). *The invented reality: How do we know what we believe we know? Contributions to constructivism.* New York: W. W. Norton.

Watzlawick, P. (1984). Self-fulfilling prophecies. In P. Watzlawick (Ed.), *The invented reality* (pp. 95–117). New York: W.W. Norton.

Watzlawick, P. (1990). *Munchhausen's pigtail.* W. W. Norton.

Watzlawick, P.A., Beavin, J.H., & Jackson, D.D. (1967). *Pragmatics of human communication.* New York: W.W. Norton.

Watzlawick, P., Weakland, J.H., & Fisch, R. (1974). *Change: Principles of problem formation and problem resolution.* New York: W.W. Norton.

Weiner, N. (1961). *Cybernetics, or control and communication in the animal and the machine.* Cambridge, MA: MIT Press.

Weiss, R.L. (1980). Strategic behavioral marital therapy: Toward a model for assessment and intervention. In J.P. Vincent (Ed.), *Advances in family intervention* (Vol. I). Greenwich, CT. JAI Press.

Whalen, C.K., & Henker, B. (1991). Therapies for hyperative children: Comparisons, combinations, and compromises. *Journal of Consulting and Clinical Psychology,* 59(1), 126–137.

Whalen, C.K., Henker, B., Hinshaw, S., Heller, T., & Huber-Dressler, A. (1991). Messages of medication: Effects of actual versus informed medication status on hyperative boys' expectancies and self-evaluations. *Journal of Consulting and Clinical Psychology,* *59*(4), 602–606.

Whitaker, C.A. & Bumberry, W.M. (1988). *Dancing with the family: A symbolic-experiential approach.* New York: Brunner/Mazel.

Whitaker, C.A., & Keith, D.V. (1981). Symbolic-experiental family therapy. In A.S. Gurman & D.P. Kniskern (Eds.), *Handbook of family therapy,* Vol I (pp. 187–225). New York: Brunner/Mazel.

Whitaker, C.A., & Malone, T.P. (1953). *The roots of psychotherapy.* New York: Blakiston.

White, M. (1986). Negative explanation, restraint, and double description: A template for family therapy. *Family Process, 25*(2), 169–184.

White, M., & Epston, D. (1990). *Narrative means to therapeutic ends.* New York: W.W. Norton.

Wynne, L.C. (1984). The epigenesis of relational systems: A model for undertaking family development. *Family Process, 23,* 297–318.

Zeig, J. (1980). *A teaching seminar with Milton H. Erickson.* New York: Brunner/Mazel.

Index